# Private Desires,
# Political Action

# Private Desires, Political Action

## An Invitation to the Politics of Rational Choice

Michael Laver

SAGE Publications

London • Thousand Oaks • New Dehli

SAGE Publications Ltd
6 Bonhill Street
London EC2A 4PU

SAGE Publications Inc
2455 Teller Road
Thousand Oaks, California 91320

SAGE Publications India Pvt Ltd
32, M-Block Market
Greater Kailash – I
New Delhi 110 048

**British Library Cataloguing in Publication data**

A catalogue record for this book is available from the British
Library

ISBN 0 7619 5114 8
ISBN 0 7619 5115 6 (pbk)

**Library of Congress catalog record available**

Typeset by Photoprint, Torquay, Devon
Printed in Great Britain by Biddles Ltd, Guildford, Surrey

# Contents

# Preface

This book started life as a massively revised edition of *The Politics of Private Desires*, originally published by Penguin Books in 1981. Revising an ancient book in a fast-moving field turned out to be a harrowing experience. This is not because there was so much new literature to refer to. There has of course been an explosion of literature in the field since 1980, when *The Politics of Private Desires* was completed but, as I make clear in the opening chapter, this is not a review of the literature. The problem was that I found, when re-reading the original book carefully for the first time in many years, that it seemed so wrong in so many places. At times I could hardly bear to read what I had written. I was tempted to run away from the revision, leaving the original text to die a decent death, but as you can see I didn't. When I came out from under the bed and had a another look, three things about *The Politics of Private Desires* did still seem as valid today as they were when it was originally written, and encouraged me to persevere.

First, rational choice theory, the real subject of the book, is still a collection of disparate writings on a varied range of matters. It thus still fails in my view, and despite its evident potential to the contrary, to exploit the fact that there are indeed unifying themes that do make it a general 'approach' to analysing politics. Despite a very welcome increase in the extent to which different parts of the approach now borrow and adapt concepts from each other there is still far too little synergy between its component parts. And I now understand much better why this is the case.

The sharp end of rational choice theory really is very sharp. Since the approach relies famously on a formal style of argument, there has been a strong tendency for practitioners to see the way forward in terms of ever-increasing technical sophistication and/or complexity. This has spawned something of a 'have gun, will travel' approach among sharp-end practitioners, as high-tech intellectual gunslingers has moved from one application in the field to another, solving one local problem before moving on quickly to another. There have been relatively few people at the cutting edge of the approach who have picked a big *substantive* problem and stuck with this over a long period of time, interpreting developments in the field as a whole in terms of how these can help them with their task. Norman Schofield's work on coalitions, developed systematically over many years, is one obvious exception to this rule. (For some reflections on this, see Schofield, 1997). Thus while there has in fact been an increasing level of *technical* cross-fertilization in the field, there has been little real cross-fertilization of *substantive* arguments. Since 1980, indeed, I have become more rather than less fearful that the entire approach is concerned far more with technique than with substance. This book, as was its predecessor, is aggressively concerned with substance rather than technique in an attempt to redress this balance.

This leads to the second theme that links this book with its ancestor, which is that the main substantive structure of the original argument remains the same. Thus each chapter deals with the same themes as before in the same logical sequence. We move from the particular and individual to the general and political, from an individual rational calculus to problems of collective action, to the role of politics in resolving those problems, building at each stage upon the arguments of the previous one. This is appropriate because the rational choice approach, as we shall see, is ultimately reductionist in its methodological insistence on deducing logical accounts of politics from assumptions about individuals.

There was a time when, if an academic colleague (most often a philosopher or sociologist) accused someone of being a reductionist then that was the end of the matter. If not actually running away and bursting into tears in some dark corner, the accused could never really dispel the suspicion that they might indeed have done something mad, bad or sad. I too was wounded by accusations of reductionism back in the early 1980s but now I can honestly say that I really do see nothing wrong with it. Many more years since then of reading volumes of 'non-reductionist' writings on politics have not convinced me of their superior virtues. Quite the contrary. At least 'reductionist' rational choice theorists typically have the intellectual toughness that comes from first defining a more or less unambiguous set of premises and then applying a system of logic more or less rigorously to these, in an attempt to generate interesting and non-obvious interpretations of the world of politics. The results of all this may be spartan but they are rarely waffle. While rational choice theorists must of course be ready, willing and able to defend themselves against rival *coherent* models of politics, they should not be embarrassed when critics claim that 'thick' description, 'rich' case studies or haphazard cross-national empirical research tell more of the truth than a coherent logical model.

In one way I have, however, pulled back from a rather grandiose objective that motivated me when I wrote *The Politics of Private Desires* in 1980. I no longer think that the rational choice approach can be knocked into a single, unified, model of politics covering everything from the moment of creation to the end of the universe. Too much blood must be shed trying to defend this position and there is really no good reason to defend it. In practical terms, however, this does not undermine the argument in the present book, which deals with a series of matters – concerning collective action and political competition – that are self-evidently interrelated. It does seem sensible to argue that theoretical accounts of these matters should hang together substantively.

The third distinctive feature of *The Politics of Private Desires* is that it was aggressively non-technical. I do not flinch one little bit from doing things the same way again. The substantive themes discussed in what follows are important matters of interest to all. There is some validity in the dismissive accusation of a number of critics that rational choice theorists spend their days in ivory towers counting how many rational angels can dance on the head of a pin, given the relative unwillingness of practitioners to express their arguments in a form that can be read, appreciated and of course criticized by outsiders, especially those who know a lot about the substance of politics. Non-technical does not mean simplistic, however, despite the occasional protestations of some of those high-tech sharp-shooters to the contrary. I hope this book is not simplistic. Its intention is to discuss, and to reflect upon, some of the main issues considered by rational choice theorists, and to suggest ways in which the whole enterprise might be moved forward. My criterion has remained that, if a substantive argument cannot adequately be discussed in words rather than mathematical formulae, then it is best left to the technocrats and, at the same time I am afraid, probably consigned to obscurity.

So much for what has stayed the same. Much, however, has changed since the original version of *The Politics of Private Desires*. As I indicated above, I found myself unwilling to stand over quite a bit of the detailed argument in the original, and have made substantial changes to this. And many good things have been published in the meantime that do of course have to be taken into account. The result is that this is in practice less of a revision of *The Politics of Private Desires* and more of a new book. It is in some sense based upon the original text, and the argument does have the same basic structure. While I have felt free to reuse the original words, nearly all of the sentences in this book differ from those in the original version and many parts have been totally rewritten from scratch. To signal that this is mostly a new book, I have given it a mostly new title, *Private Desires, Political Action*, but one which does retain the 'private desires' brand name by which the old book became known.

In terms of substance, probably the greatest changes have been made to the discussions of public goods – which I have banished almost entirely and replaced with the more general notion of 'political services' – and of political entrepreneurs. The latter still present one the great challenges for rational choice theorists since they provide a link between probably the two major sub-fields in the approach – the politics of collective action and the politics of elections and party competition. Despite the fact that not much has been written on political entrepreneurs since 1980, I remain utterly convinced of their importance. Rereading what I had written on the subject in *The Politics of Private Desires*, was a truly toe-curling experience. It is just plain silly to claim, as I did then, that politicians can be seen as people who use publicly mandated sanctions to produce public goods for profit and retain the surplus for themselves. They don't, at least legally, in any political system with which I am familiar.

I now present politicians as people who provide various services that help groups resolve collective action problems. This discussion of the role of politicians has also been helped very much by developments in various aspects of rational choice theory. The whole 'principal–agent' approach, with its focus on shirking and monitoring, has been justly influential since 1980 and does add a lot to how we can think of politicians. Much more has been written on the role of reputation, allowing us to see politicians as developing reputations that become part of their stock-in-trade and giving us an account of why it is reasonable to expect that they will do at least part of what they say they will do.

Many other detailed parts of the discussion have also changed. Developments in the discipline have forced a complete overhaul of the discussion of voting and party competition. The paradox of why people vote when their vote can't make a difference, for example, has been discussed by many more people in much more interesting ways than it had in 1980. Accounts of voting and party competition are now based on multidimensional, rather than one-dimensional descriptions of people's tastes. Discussions of the politics of coalition have become much more sophisticated in recent years and the chapter on this subject has therefore been expanded as well as overhauled from top to bottom.

But at the end of it all, this is at least the same *sort* of book as *The Politics of Private Desires*. Even if most of the words and much of the detailed argument are different, my basic motivation in writing it remains my conviction that rational choice theory has an awful lot to contribute to how we understand the political world, just as long as the real engine behind its development is a concern for the substance of politics rather than for techniques of political analysis. To find a review of some of the specific ways in which rational choice theory has made a contribution to our understanding of the real political world, readers should do now what people should always do after reading the preface of a book such as this, which is jump straight to the conclusion before reading anything else.

*The Politics of Private Desires* was in effect my first book. The original project comprised a book of words about various aspects of the politics of private desires, and an appendix of games, one game for each chapter in the book. The idea of the games was that people, in playing these, would get more of an intuitive feel for the ideas so imperfectly expressed in the words. Penguin separated the words from the games and published them separately, and the games appeared first in 1979 as *Playing Politics*. As it happens, I have also just done a massive revision of *Playing Politics*, with new games and better versions of the old games. This is appearing as *Playing Politics: the Nightmare Continues*, published by Oxford University Press. I still feel quite strongly that playing games such as these can give people a much more subtle intuitive feel for the ideas so imperfectly expressed in words or even, dare I say it, in mathematical formulae.

Finally, I should thank many people. First, there is Ziyad Marar of Sage, who suggested publishing a revised edition of *The Politics of Private Desires* (though I must say I did not always thank him in my heart when facing the actual task of revision). Then there are Thad Brown, Ricca Edmondson, Eddie Hyland, Peter Morriss, Ken Shepsle and Kaare Strom who went in detail through an earlier draft of this revised book, between them bringing the skills of political scientist and political philosopher to bear upon it and suggesting ways in which the whole thing might be made less awful. Getting a fat typescript from a 'friend' in the profession and being asked for sensible comments on it is an occupational hazard but it is not something, if we are honest, that any of us much relish. So these thanks really are heartfelt, as are my apologies for wantonly ignoring some of this good advice, even when it was right. Finally and most importantly, there are so many friends and colleagues with whom I have discussed the world over the years. I am not going to name names for that would be invidious, although I can certainly trace particular pieces of the argument that follows to particular conversations I have had with particular people. Some of the people involved, if they read this book, may well recognize those conversations too. The bottom line is that every idea in this book has developed from an interaction of some sort with a friend, enemy and/or intellectual colleague. It is customary at this point to reserve all of the blame for oneself, but I have never been wholly convinced, when friends, enemies and colleagues have contributed so much to my thinking, that they can so easily be exonerated.

Michael Laver, Dalkey, September 1996

# 1

# Introduction

## The politics of private desires

This book is about the political consequences of private desires. It presents
an interpretation of the political world that is based upon the assumption that
people get involved in politics in order to further their own personal
objectives.

While such a view of the world may seem to leave little room for the
politics of altruism and self-sacrifice, this is not as depressing as it might
seem at first sight, for two main reasons. First, I set firmly on one side the
issue of where people's objectives might actually come from. I certainly do
not believe in original sin, but I do leave the 'nature versus nurture'
argument about the sources of our private desires to the realms of sociology
and psychology, two fields in which I have little or no expertise. Second, the
entire discussion in this book is something of a mind game that does not
necessarily purport to deal with the world as it actually is (whatever that
might be). The rules of this game are quite simple. Assume for the sake of
argument that people participate in politics to fulfil their private desires; then
build a theoretical model of what the world of politics would look like if this
were indeed the case.

If the model world we build looks even a little bit like the real world in
which most of us live and breathe every day, then this surely provides us
with some interesting food for thought. Our model world might of course
look like the real world for entirely accidental reasons, but then again it
might not. The similarities between our model and reality may well suggest
that self-interest really is an important feature of the cut and thrust of day-to-
day politics. If we do decide to play along with the assumption that politics
has a lot to do with self-interest, then we can use our model in all sorts of
interesting ways to explore how the real political world might possibly
work.

Of course a model of the world is not at all the same as the real thing. It
is an incredibly simplistic abstraction from reality. Any description of the
world, whether in a newspaper article, a novel, a painting, a ballet, a TV
soap opera or a political theory, is bound to be incomplete. At best such
descriptions can contain no more than a few nuggets of insight into how the
world actually works. Each type of description has its own virtues that may
or may not make up for its inevitable massive shortcomings. The virtues of
using a theoretical model to describe political systems, for example, derive
from the ways in which such a model allows us systematically to manipulate

various features of this world, in order to see what happens when we do this. We can even play with our model to explore what might happen in 'counter-factual' situations that have never yet, and perhaps never will, come to pass. We can thus use a model to conduct experiments that would be considered to be the very height of irresponsibility if we were to try them out on an actual political system that had a major impact on the lives of human beings who live, love, love life and don't like to be experimented upon.

This way of studying politics has become quite common over the past couple of decades, especially in an intellectual tradition led by a group of authors who are usually described as 'rational choice theorists', although it is important to note that the concept of rationality that these theorists use has a special, technical, meaning. In common usage we usually praise someone by calling them rational, and criticize them by calling them irrational. The technical use of the concept of 'rationality', however, makes no such value judgements. It is applied strictly to 'goal-seeking behaviour'. This is behaviour, however bizarre it might seem to an outsider, that is intended to fulfil certain desires, however base these desires might appear to the rest of the world. In contrast to what is typically a rather looser popular usage, no judgement at all is made by rational choice theorists about the substance of these desires. The label 'rational choice theory' is therefore confusing for all but the *cognoscenti* but, like many confusing labels, it is widely used. I would only compound matters by trying to change it, but please remember throughout that the notion of rationality that is used in this book has a special technical meaning.

Rational choice theories, not to mention rational choice theorists, often intimidate or even horrify innocent bystanders, borrowing extensively as they do from economics, formal logic and sometimes also mathematics. To be sure, rational choice theorists tend to be people with strong stomachs who do not flinch from reading and writing complicated-looking equations. Some, sad to say, positively relish rendering their arguments as complex and technical as possible, making their theories look like the formulae that describe the construction of a thermonuclear warhead or an apple. The hearts inside such breasts do beat a little faster when highly intelligent colleagues can make neither head nor tail of what is being said. Rational choice theorists often communicate with each other in an ugly and arcane language that mixes English, Greek and mathematics, a language designed neither to enrich our aesthetic lives nor to reach out and welcome the uninitiated.

Actually, there is nothing inherently mathematical about the rational choice approach. It does depend, however, upon the rigorous application of logic to precisely defined assumptions and for this reason can sometimes be taxing and complex. This book, which I must confess is to a large extent about rational choice theory, seeks to reach out and welcome all comers. For this reason I turn my back on quasi-mathematical formulations, in order to confine any brain-strain to the real political issues with which we should be concerned and to make arguments about these as widely accessible as possible. I use words and sentences throughout, banish symbols more or less entirely and will take my chances with the purists. An occasionally distressing consequence of this is that the words and sentences are from time to time rather long and cumbersome, for which I apologize most sincerely in advance.

Rational choice techno-jocks will smile triumphantly as I say this, pointing out as politely as they are able that real politics is actually much more complicated than a thermonuclear warhead or an apple. They will then reaffirm resolutely that their highly evolved symbolic language helps them not only to avoid those long and ugly sentences (indeed to avoid any sentences whatsoever in a few cases) but at the same time to be very precise. Of course they are right. For the truly tiny proportion of the world's population who can actually understand what they are saying, what they are saying makes a lot of sense.

But this book is not a Luddite tract, far from it. There is quite definitely a crucial role in political science for sharp-end rational choice theorists. Indeed some of the most spectacular innovations in post-war political science have been made by such people. And it is quite false to claim, just because an ordinary decent human being can be blown up by a thermonuclear warhead or sink her teeth deep into an apple without having the faintest idea about what goes on inside, that nobody needs a deep technical understanding of how these things work. The sad thing about how the rational choice approach has developed, given this great potential, is that its powerful *and simple* insights tend to get lost in the thickets of equations that characterize writing that is sometimes more concerned with technical fireworks than with bringing an analytical searchlight to bear upon matters of real substance.

## Models of politics

The rational choice approach to analysing politics actually comprises a collection of different 'theories' about various aspects of political life. The rather coy quotation marks I am using are intended to indicate that these 'theories' are different from those with which many will be familiar.

The theories we will be considering in this book are characterized by a distinctive approach to constructing an argument. They start with a set of *a priori*, or 'primitive', assumptions, definitions and concepts that are in some sense logically distinct from the phenomenon with which the analyst is concerned. The implications of these assumptions are unfolded in a systematic and logical manner in an attempt to throw light upon the phenomenon under investigation. The primitives that ground the model may be statements about how the world actually is. Or they may be purely speculative conjectures. Indeed one of the joys of the approach is that I can make any *a priori* assumptions I want when I construct a rational choice model of politics. There is absolutely no reason, for example, why I should not assume that the world is inhabited by beautiful and generous people concerned only with the welfare of others. I could easily construct a theoretical model that unfolded the logical implications of this *a priori* assumption, among others. Its empirical plausibility would be neither here nor there when we came to evaluate the logical coherence of the model.

*The essential purpose of the rational choice approach is thus to construct a logically coherent potential explanation of the phenomenon under investigation.* Empirical validity is always welcome, of course, but it is not the primary motivation. Indeed a primary virtue of the rational choice approach is its ability to deal with 'counter-factual' situations that have never (yet) come to pass.

Rational choice models of politics can therefore be used to do two things. First, and in my view most importantly, they can be manipulated logically in an attempt to produce helpful and/or provocative interpretations that may deepen and broaden our understanding of real politics. These interpretations can also be applied to hypothetical and counter-factual situations in an attempt to explore the potential of any particular situation, as well as more fanciful political futures. Rational choice models have, in my view at least, helpfully and provocatively expanded our understanding of politics in a wide range of fields. There can be little doubt that we now understand much more about collective action, about the potential inconsistencies and instabilities associated with majority decision-making, and about coalition bargaining, than we did before rational choice theorists got to work on these important topics.

Second, they may be used to generate explicit propositions about real world phenomena, propositions that we can compare with what actually happens and in this sense 'test', in order to derive some sort of feel for the general empirical plausibility of the argument in question. If our logic is flawless, then such 'tests' are in fact evaluations of our assumptions, the veracity and completeness of which can often be assessed only indirectly. If our assumptions are correct, then such 'tests' are instead evaluations of our logic, although this logic is probably better evaluated directly, on the basis of careful and rigorous thought. Rational choice models of the formation of coalition governments, for example, have been subjected over the years to a wide range of empirical tests. Several of these models have been shown to add significantly to our ability to forecast the composition of coalition governments in the real world.

These features of rational choice models are in contrast to the methodological style of the more empirical approach to 'theory' that characterizes much of the rest of the modern political science literature. The more empirical approach sets out to generate hypotheses about real world political interactions by making systematic observations of what real people actually do, guided in what, precisely, to observe by common sense and the reported results of previous research. Having made such observations, the analyst attempts to generalize these into more overarching propositions about how the world works. These propositions are evaluated in terms of how well they correspond to a completely new set of observations of the world. These new data, in theory at least, are collected quite independently of the research that generated the overarching propositions in the first place.

*The essential purpose of the more empirical approach to political science is thus to generate plausible and robust general statements that are consistent with observed empirical patterns.* Analysts will always look for a causal structure in these patterns, of course, but observed patterns in the data are what drive this search, not the logical structure of the explanation that might underlie these.

An example from the physical world may serve to illustrate the distinction between the *a priori* and the empirical approaches to modelling. Imagine we wanted to be able to predict at what time the sun would rise on every morning of the year at some important point on the globe, say Dalkey, Co. Dublin. We could proceed in two ways.

The empirical way would be to record the time of sunrise in Dalkey every morning until we felt we could decode the pattern of times that we observed. If we were smart this would take much less than a full year, though it would probably take about three months until we were able to get a firm enough idea of the pattern of sunrises to allow us to project from this into the future. If we are prepared to assume that sunrises next year will follow the same pattern as sunrises this year, then we can generalize from our observed pattern of Dalkey sunrises to make predictions about the time of sunrise in Dalkey on any particular date next year. And, when next year comes around, we can put these predictions to the test.

We might be able in this way to construct an empirical 'model' that could forecast the time of sunrises in Dalkey very accurately indeed, without ever really getting to the bottom of what was causing these, without ever really *understanding* what is going on. Indeed we could even do so while systematically *misunderstanding* what is going on, but doing so in a manner that is consistent with our observations. (We might conclude that the sun rotates around the earth rather than vice versa, for example.) This might not cause us any problems as long as all of the factors conditioning our observations remained the same. If we spent our whole lives in Dalkey for example, then we might never realize that we were quite unable to predict the times of sunrises in Honolulu or indeed in any other location significantly closer to the equator. If by some chance we did move to Honolulu, then we would find ourselves completely in the dark about when the sun might rise, and would almost certainly have to repeat our extensive empirical researches before we could get a grip on this.

An alternative way of doing things would be to think long and hard about *why* it is that the sun rises every morning and sets every evening, at a different time each day. At the end of a marathon thinking session we might come up with a logical model of the solar system, built from a set of *a priori* assumptions about how the world works. The model might even have a physical manifestation. We might for example construct a set of ivory balls sliding on bronze orbits that we could crank round and round the sun by turning a finely carved ebony handle connected to an elegantly jewelled gearing mechanism. Or our model might have a purely logical existence – being built into a computer program, or even inside our own brains. If we get the model right, we gain a good understanding of the rising and setting of the sun, and may even be able to use it to predict actual sunrises.

Note, however, that the physical model of the solar system that we built in our workshop and then cranked around the sun might be rather rough and ready at such predictions. It might be a beautiful and sophisticated construction, a fantastic tool for adding to our understanding of the world, but might not be very good at predicting the time, to the nearest second, that the sun will rise in Dalkey, or indeed in Honolulu, on 3 August in the year 2001.

Thus raw predictive success is not the be-all and end-all of evaluating any model. Despite its vague and inaccurate predictions, our mechanical model that cranked the planets around the sun would be much more versatile in a range of different settings than a mere list of sunrises in Dalkey, for example. We could use it to make a stab at forecasting the sunrise in Honolulu, the North Pole, or indeed anywhere in the world, any day of the year, without having to hop on a plane, book into a luxury hotel, stay for months and months and make loads of new observations. Our model, if it was less than absolutely perfect, would make somewhat inaccurate predictions, but these would be far, far better than operating on the basis that the sun will rise on the North Pole at the same time as it rises in Dalkey. Even more intriguingly, we could crank the model backwards, and see what would happen if the earth went round the sun in the opposite direction. Indeed we could tinker with the model in all sorts of ways, making the earth a bit bigger or tilting it more on its axis, for example, and in this way answer many interesting 'what if' questions that we could never come to grips with on the basis of direct empirical observation.

The crucial characteristic of the *a priori* approach is thus the generation of interesting and non-obvious statements about the world from a set of assumptions and a system of logic. In the strict sense of the word, therefore, rational choice theories should be 'tautological' – their conclusions entirely determined by the assumptions and system of logic that they use. The word 'tautological' is commonly and inaccurately used as a term of abuse in academic circles, rather than in its strict sense as something of a compliment. It often wrongly serves as a synonym for 'boring' or 'trivial'. Despite this, the purpose of rational choice theory is the search for *interesting and non-trivial* tautological arguments.

This means that the criteria for evaluating rational choice models are rather different from those used to judge more conventional empirical approaches. For the latter, we tend to explore the robustness of their empirical generalizations about the real world. For rational choice models, we tend to make judgements on the basis of what we think about their assumptions and their internal logic. If you find a model's assumptions interesting and/or stimulating, its logic sound and its implications to be more than trivial, then you will find that a rational choice model may increase your understanding of the world. You will feel that in this sense it has some 'heuristic' value. If you find its assumptions preposterous and pointless, its logic faulty, and its implications either banal or just plain wrong, then you will see no reason at all to take it seriously.

There are, of course, some rather less subjective principles that guide us when evaluating any model, including any rational choice model. A model is better if it is reasonably *parsimonious* – doing its job using as few, and as simple, steps as possible to build upon assumptions that are as straightforward, and uncontentious, as possible.

All models are more interesting and useful if they apply to *general* problems, rather than to something very specific – a 'model' that is so specific that it applies only to a single case at a single point of time is after all not really a model at all, but a redescription of the case at issue. Other things being equal, therefore, a model that can be used in a variety of different situations is better than one that works only in very special circumstances.

In addition to being parsimonious and general, the best models make relatively *precise*, rather than relatively vague, statements about the world. After all, a model of sunrises that says that the sun will either rise or set or do neither of these things some time or other this evening is bound to be accurate, but is clearly of little practical use.

One reason for looking favourably upon precise predictions bears upon yet another criterion for evaluating models, which is their empirical accuracy. Models can, either directly or indirectly, be used to generate statements about the real world. These statements can then be evaluated in terms of their empirical validity. It should be clear to anyone who has been reading between the lines that my own view is that the strict empirical accuracy of forecasts generated by any rational choice model is secondary to the value of the model in expanding our understanding of the world. Nevertheless, other things being equal, it is obviously useful to construct at least some of our models on the basis of plausible, rather than implausible, assumptions. For this reason, we should not turn our backs on the empirical evaluation of propositions derived from our models.

There are, therefore, some general standards that we can bring to bear upon the job of evaluating theoretical models, but at the same time we should not be slaves to these. The real bottom line for any model is whether or not we find it useful and illuminating. Even a model that fails some of the tests set out above can add greatly to our understanding, although we must then face up to the issue of how to separate the good models from the bad ones.

In the end, the criteria we in practice use to evaluate the usefulness of a model are very subjective, and this is in somewhat paradoxical contrast to the apparent rigour of the models themselves. In the real world people take up and use models that they like and find useful, as long as these have no glaring logical errors. They ignore models that they don't like or find useless, despite the fact that these may be awesome logical constructions. This is as it should be, for a model of the political world is no more than a tool to help us expand our understanding. And we use those tools that we find useful, leaving on the shelf those that we do not. Your choice of which model to use for a particular job is, provided the model you choose is not inherently faulty, ultimately a matter of taste.

## Rational choice models of politics

The rational choice approach thus comprises a collection of different theories about various aspects of political life, held together by the methodo-logical similarities that we have just discussed. While these theories may be eminently rigorous and consistent as far as their *internal* logic is concerned, any consistency *between* theories is largely a matter of luck. Exhaustive, and sometimes exhausting, explorations of the full range of logical possibilities produced by a given set of assumptions has often resulted in interesting and provocative conclusions about some particular political process. The sum total of all this endeavour is a collection of writers and writings that does, in practical terms, amount to a school, a paradigm or a tradition. The problem is that, if we take each of these theories in turn and classify its premises and purpose, we find no obvious reason why the group of theories as a whole should logically fit together.

For example, it does not take us long to identify a number of interesting sub-species of human being. These range from the person in the jungle to the person in the street, to the voter, the party activist, the politician, the idealist, the megalomaniac and even, on occasion, the altruist. We might want to explain a certain phenomenon, such as turning out to vote at elections. We see that a voter receives little in return for the costs of voting that can be denominated in terms of worn shoe leather, lost time and mental distress, among many other things. We therefore invoke such motivations as 'the satisfaction of complying with the ethic of voting' or 'civic duty' (matters to which we will return at some length). In contrast, when explaining other forms of participation such as belonging to a trade union or a consumer group, we scratch our heads and puzzle about the 'collective action problem' (another thorny topic to which we shall be returning), when invoking 'civic duty' would solve the problem at a stroke.

In order to reconcile different rational choice theories that deal with various aspects of politics, I shall attempt to describe them in the following chapters as if they had all been derived from a common set of 'core' *a priori* assumptions. Much more controversially, I am going to apply a rather rigid criterion to the assumptions that I will allow into this core set: I shall include only those assumptions about the fundamental intrinsic motivations of individuals which can be precisely defined with reference to a single individual, as opposed to a collection of individuals. In short, I will allow into the core set of assumptions only *asocial* statements about the motiva-tions of individuals.

Once more this is less stark than it might seem at first sight, since it certainly does not preclude people from having all sorts of social motivations that derive from the core set of assumptions. As we shall see quite shortly, and as most of us know anyway, we all have desires that we cannot realize on our own, so that much of our behaviour is social. But the fact remains that the primitive motivational assumptions that will be allowed into the core set, and which are assumed to motivate these more social desires, will relate to the individual as a self-contained unit of analysis.

The set of core assumptions will therefore describe something like an asocial 'state of nature'. The state-of-nature technique has undergone a minor renaissance following the publication of very widely read and cited works by Robert Nozick (1974) and John Rawls (1972). It is, in my view, a very useful device for ensuring that, whatever their plausibility, the theories we consider produce accounts of the political realm that are not trivial. While the state-of-nature device is not an integral part of the rational choice method itself, it provides a very powerful criterion for maintaining the distinctive character and explanatory power of this general approach to modelling political interactions.

Nozick's methodological assertion, and it is no more than an assertion, is that this approach enables us to generate 'fundamental potential explanations' of the political realm. These explanations are 'fundamental' in the sense that they are based on assumptions defined in a different realm from the realm of the process to be explained, and they are 'potential' in the sense that, if the assumptions were correct and the logic sound, they would indeed be accurate explanations of what was going on. Such explanations are interesting, even if their assumptions are found to be untenable since, according to Nozick (who was interested among other things in accounting for the emergence of the state), '[w]e learn much by seeing how the state could have arisen, even if it didn't arise that way. If it didn't arise that way, we would also learn much by determining why it didn't: by trying to explain why the particular bit of the real world that deviates from the state-of-nature model is as it is' (1974: 9).

The implicit assumption in this argument is that explanations of phenomena in one realm (the political), on the basis of motivational assumptions defined entirely in another realm (the individual), are somehow 'deeper' than explanations of the political in terms only of the political. And, if a model is to have any value at all, it must in some important sense be deeper and more general than any social setting with which it deals. While I am not totally convinced by Nozick's arguments about the role of fundamental potential explanations, and while if you fed me enough Navy rum I might concede that real people do sometimes have very basic social motivations, I am very much convinced that the value of rational choice models is greatly enhanced if they continually strive to construct fundamental potential explanations.

This is because of the real dangers involved in *not* doing so. Once we allow the possibility that individuals have *intrinsic motivations for particular forms of social interaction*, then any problem we encounter when modelling social interaction can be 'solved' by imagining some individual who has just the right social motivation for the problem at hand. Of course, altruists and secular saints, motivated solely by the desire to have everyone interact productively and peacefully with one another, may actually ride to our rescue in particular situations. But we must construct models of politics to be robust to many general possibilities, not to work only if a specific person rides conveniently to the rescue.

Without wishing to give too much away at this stage, a quick example might clarify the point. Consider possible interpretations of a political phenomenon such as voting, an act that we have already argued has some costs for each individual but which has little chance of having any measurable effect. We have seen that some theorists set out to explain voting in terms of motivations such as 'civic duty' – in effect, they explain voting by saying that people vote because they want to (in the sense that they are motivated to fulfil what they see as their 'duty'). In the end we (at least I) feel somewhat dissatisfied with this explanation. Something seems to be missing. We are explaining a political act with a socially determined motivation and somehow we don't seem to have gone deep enough.

We might go one stage further and look at the sanctions that might be applied to people who do not fulfil their civic duty – perhaps people who shirk their duty by not voting will be ostracized by others, at some cost to both the shirkers and to those who ostracize them. We are getting a little deeper, but why would people ostracize others who failed to fulfil their civic duty, since ostracizing people has costs too? Perhaps they do this because they feel that, as soon as one person gets away with shirking their civic duty, then others will also try to do so, and everyone will ultimately end up being worse off. At this level, the individually costly act of ostracizing a shirker may be seen to have direct and measurable individual benefits, and we may feel that our explanation is beginning to bite. We are actually using our argument to get from one place, the individual realm, to another, the world of social action, and in consequence we may feel that we have achieved something.

An alternative method of confronting the same problem would be to adopt a quite different, and more empirical, approach to generating hypotheses about the world. We could observe the characteristics that appeared in the real world to be related to turning out to vote, and try to make some sense out of these. If a perfect piece of empirical research could be conducted on this subject, it could quite possibly provide a plausible and interesting account of voting turnout. This account might even enable us to predict turnout in future elections and, in its own terms, would be an eminently respectable piece of work.

The empirical approach would not, however, enable us to explore all the possibilities, the prime virtue of an *a priori* model. The empirically derived account *in the last analysis* more or less says that the world is as it is because that is how it is, although theory is not theory at all without interesting and plausible explanations of the relationship between the various component parts of the whole to be explained. The problem with a model using a purely empirical approach to deriving generalizations about the world is that it does not in any systematic way go deeper than the observed patterns of social interaction that represent the model's building blocks.

I regard the clinching argument in favour of the use of fundamental potential explanations, or something like them, to be the need to maintain a firm distinction between empirical and *a priori* ways of doing things. It is clear that these alternative approaches should not be employed simultaneously. If, in the same account of politics, we alternate *a priori* and empirical methodologies, then we greatly undermine the value of our explanation, reducing it to little more than a rationalization of the world as it actually is. A number of rational choice theorists have fallen into this trap, starting with a set of *a priori* motivational assumptions, arriving at a point where their deductions seriously diverge from observed reality, and solving their problems at a stroke by switching into the empirical mode of analysis. They use their empirical findings to modify their *a prioris* in such a way as to allow them to deduce observed reality, and then proceed blithely on their way as if nothing at all had happened.

If we change our assumptions every time we get stuck we can of course explain absolutely anything. This is very convenient but rather unsatisfying, since rational choice theory becomes little more than the rationalization of choice. The use of fundamental potential explanations does not, of course, automatically eliminate this possibility, but it does serve two useful functions. In the first place, it makes the analyst more aware of what is being attempted at each stage of the explanatory process. Furthermore, the introduction of new, socially defined, *a prioris* is often the most tempting and damaging response for an analyst faced with a divergence between rational choice models and reality.

It is important to notice that I am not claiming that 'the social whole is no more than the sum of its individual parts'. While I shall insist that fundamental motivational assumptions are defined entirely in terms of individuals, secondary motivational assumptions, such as the desire to participate, may be deduced from these, and may make sense only in relation to a group of individuals. Furthermore, many of the definitions and concepts used will only make sense when applied to collectivities. Much of the discussion in this book, for example, is concerned with the concept of collective action. If there was only one individual in the whole world, then the concept of collective action would obviously make no sense. The theories I discuss, therefore, are not totally reductionist, although they come quite close to being so; we should be under no illusions about that. The many disadvantages of reductionist methodologies must be acknowledged, and offset against the advantages that can be gained from them, in heuristic terms as well as in terms of increased coherence and rigour. At this level, all rational choice theories are necessarily reductionist in their attempt to deduce explanations of political processes from assumptions about individual motivations. The approach adopted in this book therefore presents no new problems in this respect. It merely represents an attempt to extract the maximum heuristic advantage in exchange for the inevitable shortcomings of this methodology.

## Rational choice theory and political science

Rational choice theory itself has become the subject of vigorous and interesting debate, a product no doubt of the approach's successful colonization of various important corners of political science. Earlier critiques tended to concentrate on what were seen, almost certainly correctly, as the individualist, reductionist and economistic orientations of rational choice theory. This debate has more or less died down as people who don't like the approach for these reasons have responded, quite rightly in their own terms given the relative inaccessibility of most of the literature, by ignoring it as a wrongheaded but ultimately harmless exercise in needless formalization. Similarly, rational choice theorists in political science, again in their own terms for perfectly good reasons, have seen little mileage in getting drawn into ideological debates with those outside the field when their primary aim (unlike some of their intellectual cousins in departments of economics) is not to promote an ideological world-view but rather to unpack the implications of an intriguing and suggestive logical model that may offer useful intuitions about important political processes in the real world.

In some ways this 'modest' response on the part of rational choice theorists does not sit very easily with an approach that begins with fundamental assumptions about the thought processes of human beings, sets them in a state of nature, and deduces interpretations of the structure of some of the most basic human interactions from these premises. What can see here is a paradox within the field that has been little remarked upon. This is that an approach with such fundamental, not to say grandiose, premises seems to have been used in practice to develop, not a grand theory of the world, but a collection of middle-level theories that set out to explain a series of admittedly important and pervasive, but ultimately rather prosaic, political interactions such as collective action, voting, party competition, government formation, and so on. Starting from the same intellectual high ground as the world's great ideologies, rational choice theorists seem quickly to have retreated to the more comfortable valleys, leaving the commanding heights and big questions to be puzzled over by philosophers, sociologists and poets.

There are two responses to this. The first response is a pragmatic defence of middle-level theory in general rather than rational choice theory in particular. It argues that, while the big ideological and philosophical questions clearly are important and we should certainly not be blind to them, they are not the only important questions that we should address. Matters such as collective action, voting, party competition and government formation are important too – indeed they are even important for people who might actually want to implement their preferred solutions to the 'bigger' ideological questions. Since the big questions will never be answered definitively, it is simply silly to wait for all the answers before pressing on with the business of middle-level theory.

The second response is more specific to rational choice theory and derives from the fact that one of the canons of the approach is a style of reasoning that puts a heavy premium on being as rigorous and explicit as possible in the way we develop our arguments about political processes from fundamental premises. More than most other types of middle-level political science theorizing, therefore, the rational choice approach values being explicit about logical premises. And it values generating interpretations of phenomena in one realm of human interaction from premises grounded in another realm. Such logical primitives can for this reason look general and grandiose, but the fundamental motivation for this is methodological rigour rather than some more elevated ideological project. Of course, when they construct their middle-level theories in this way, rational choice theorists may well buy inadvertently into an ideological framework that they neither see nor agree with. But in a broad sense this is not only inevitable but can be said of all social scientists when they lower their sights from the really big questions – it is not a problem confined to rational choice theory. It only becomes a problem when a rational choice theorist behaves as if he or she is right and everyone else is wrong – which does alas happen, although fortunately not too often.

In the end, both rational choice theorists and their ideological critics have probably come to see the former as boffins playing in an intellectual sand pit of their own construction. The main difference between them is that the rational choice theorists contend that important insights into the real world can be gained in that sand pit. In doing so they appeal to what I have described as the 'heuristic' value of all good models in giving us a feel for the ways of the world. At this point there is no way of resolving the debate since, while we might just be able to come to some form of agreement about how to assess the scientific or logical merit of an argument, what is heuristically valuable for one person can easily seem either obscure or trivial to another. The heuristic value of anything, almost though not quite by definition, is very much a matter of taste.

Recently, debates on rational choice theory have confronted the approach much more on its own terms, reflecting its move to a position at least a little bit closer to the mainstream of political science. There has thus been more vigorous debate about the substance, as opposed to the very fact, of rational choice theory. Rational choice theorists certainly do not solve all the puzzles that they set themselves. While some of these failures may be the result of tackling the wrong puzzles, critics within political science argue that there are failures that do indeed call into question the current orientation of the entire field. Two recent works are especially worthy of mention at this point; I will be returning to both.

Robert Nozick's book, *The Nature of Rationality* (1993), offers a superbly rich and subtle philosophical discussion of rationality that certainly does not take the rather spartan instrumental utility-maximizing notion of rationality deployed by most rational choice theorists as the be-all and end-all of rational decision-making. Nozick explores the meaning of rational decision-making, rational belief and rational goals in an accessible, thought-provoking and very constructive way in this book. It is required and salutary reading for anyone interested in this field, mainly because Nozick really does understand what rational choice theorists are trying to do, even if he regards what at least some of them actually do as being absurdly simplistic. Since Nozick is a philosopher (as we political scientists say) the broader notions of rationality he discusses may well leave too many issues open to allow for the development of rigorous yet operational middle level theories about real political processes. Nonetheless his discussion forces rational choice theorists to face crucial questions that most of them rarely think about, and for this reason will hopefully serve to knock a bit of sense into those more enthusiastic members of the field who believe that they have discovered the one true faith.

Green and Shapiro's critique, *Pathologies of Rational Choice Theory* (1994), comes four square from within political science and has caused quite a stir in the profession. Their essential argument is that rational choice theory, despite its theoretical sophistication, has been of little empirical use: 'the empirical contributions of rational choice theory . . . are few, far between, and considerably more modest than the combination of mystique and methodological fanfare surrounding the rational choice movement would lead one to suspect' (Green and Shapiro, 1994: 179). Those political scientists who have always hated rational choice theory for one reason or another have rallied gleefully around this claim, seeing it as evidence that they were right all along not to torment themselves with all those ugly formulae and concentrate instead upon nice books full of words. Rational choice theorists themselves have been defensive and even somewhat grumpy about this, no doubt looking with suspicion at the motives of those who cite Green and Shapiro with approval, and have tended to regard the critique as hostile and unhelpful.

Both are wrong, in my view. Green and Shapiro do not dismiss rational choice theory out of hand and are clearly sympathetic to much of what it is about. Furthermore they are simply quite right that, to date, empirical applications in the field have been decidedly unimpressive. But this says as much about systematic empirical research in political science as it does about rational choice theory. To be sure, sharp-end rational choice theorists, for reasons that have never been entirely clear to me, have as a matter of fact been rather uninterested in the heavy-duty empirical testing of their models. Indeed much of the empirical evidence they have adduced, when they have adduced any empirical evidence at all, has been unsystematic, anecdotal and in this sense quite out of character with the rigour of their theoretical models. Much of the problem of poor empirical performance alluded to by Green and Shapiro, however, derives from the very virtue of rational choice theory. This is that it does tend to be rigorous theory, generating well-specified propositions that with the appropriate evidence can be determined as being either true or false, in a discipline in which much of the other theorizing is imprecise, casual, *ad hoc* and therefore much easier to find some sort of generalized empirical support for.

We should listen to Green and Shapiro and try much harder to generate rational choice models that are empirically relevant, of course. But we should not do this by sacrificing the rigour of the approach in a quest for models that are vaguer, softer and, for this reason, harder to prove wrong. This takes us into quite a different realm from the subject matter of this book. The bottom line for our purposes is that rational choice models do as well, empirically, as most other *rigorous and well-specified* models in political science, when it comes to the business of empirical evaluation. As Green and Shapiro exhort us, this is a very good reason to try our utmost to do better.

## Plan of campaign

In one sense, rational choice theory has become a victim of its own success, generating an eclectic and explosively expanding literature of variable quality. Interestingly, and to some extent vindicating the canons of the approach, it is rare for published work in the field to be obviously 'wrong'. Low-quality rational choice theory tends to be thus because it is trivial, dreary, irrelevant or, most frequently, because it uses a giant analytical sledgehammer to smash a tiny substantive nut. Rational choice theorists have however produced interesting and provocative work on many matters at the heart of modern politics, including party competition, voting, government formation, collective action, bargaining, international relations, military and nuclear strategy.

This book is not a review of the literature. For those looking for a systematic introduction to the field, Shepsle and Bonchek (1997) have recently produced an accessible primer, *Analysing Politics*, that does an excellent job of guiding interested readers through at least some of the foothills of this literature. Their book also allows those who might want to do so, and who are prepared to engage in some basic analytical training, to establish a base camp from which to attack some of rational choice theory's more dizzy heights.

What I set out below, in contrast, is less of an introduction and more of an essay that attempts to construct a general overview of a selection of disparate writings on rational choice theory in order to show that this approach, taken as a whole, might provide a coherent interpretation of competition in modern political systems. In line with my earlier comments on the technicality of much of the recent literature, this essay is also an attempt to reorient rational choice theory away from technique and back towards some of the substance of politics in the real world.

A central theme of this book has to do with such a key substantive issue: the need to reconcile the incentives towards collective action facing members of any group of rational people with the incentives for those same people, as individuals, to look after their own private interests. The nature of these conflicting incentives is discussed in Chapter 2, in which other core assumptions are also defined. In Chapter 3, we move on to consider the problems created by the need for collective action. The collective action problem defines a central paradox generated by our individualistic motivational assumptions. If a group of rational people behave so as to maximize their individual welfare, then they produce a state of affairs that is worse for each of them, *individually*, than if they had adopted more co-operative behaviour.

This paradox is so central that it is presented by some as a major justification for the role of the state, which is seen as being necessary in order to force people to co-operate 'for their own good'. The state fulfils, for some authors, a role rather like that of the Hobbesian sovereign, bringing about peace and productivity rather than a destructive war of all against all. The collective action problem has interesting consequences for even the most hard-core opponents of the role of the state, however, reconciling most of them to the need for at least some state intervention in certain spheres of social life. In Chapter 3, we also explore the anarchist argument that the things that people want, even things that they cannot be prevented from consuming, may be produced in certain circumstances without state intervention. The 'certain circumstances' in which this solution works are very much those we might expect to be preconditions for an anarchist way of doing things. Groups of individuals must be small and stable, members must be relatively far-sighted, and must have relatively equal access to resources.

This suggests – doing considerable violence to the spirit of the various authors' arguments – that we can represent the anarchist 'solution' as an interpretation of the way in which many collective action problems are in practice resolved, *even within a modern state*. Adherence to norms and values, for example, is rarely enforced by governments, but does provide valuable public benefits that can be privately enjoyed by many people. Thus there is no law that compels us to wait in line at bus queues, but we all 'anarchistically' agree to do this, even on those occasions when we might want to barge in at the front of the queue. We already regulate large areas of our social life along 'anarchistic' lines.

An alternative solution to certain collective problems may be provided by a *political entrepreneur*, who organizes various forms of collective endeavour on behalf of the group. Political entrepreneurs have been rather neglected by rational choice theorists in particular and political scientists in general, despite the fact that they are the basic actors in the development of any system of party competition, and despite the fact that party competition itself is a mainstream concern, both of rational choice theory and of political science. Our discussion, in Chapter 4, of political entrepreneurs suggests a reorientation of conventional theories of party competition, placing more emphasis on the different and potentially conflicting incentives facing entrepreneurs, as well as on the logic that leads to the formation of *political parties*. Rational choice theory often presents political parties as unitary actors, but the approach adopted in this book is to explore their evolution as alliances of political entrepreneurs offering to supply bundles of 'political services' to the public at large.

Political parties compete with each other for public support, often in practice measured in terms of votes at elections. The logic of voting decisions by members of the public is explored in Chapter 5, and the logic of competition between parties for votes in Chapter 6. In Chapter 7, we look at what happens after elections, and specifically at how alliances, or coalitions, of parties might attempt to gain control in incumbency in circumstances in which no single party is in a position to do this on its own. Once more, theories of coalition formation illustrate an odd omission in the work of many rational choice theorists. While 'coalition theory' itself is one of the boom industries in the discipline, rational choice theories of party competition and of coalition formation have for the most part been developed with scant regard for one another. Yet it is clear that the formation of party coalitions will play an important part in electoral competition between political parties, and vice versa.

Overall, the intention of this book is to present a part of rational choice theory as at least potentially a coherent whole rather than a collection of disparate parts. I have found that the most interesting consequence of this endeavour has been the need to produce sometimes rather substantial revisions of various theories in order to fit them together. The most critical phase of the argument is almost certainly the reconciliation of the collective action problem with theories of party competition, and it is here that I find the revisions of the existing theories and the role of political entrepreneurs to be most interesting. The most problematic phase of the argument concerns the behaviour of voters in large electorates. I have a feeling that this reflects the relative weakness of the rational choice approach in explaining many forms of mass behaviour, a theme to which I will return in my conclusions.

# 2
# Rational Actors

We begin with two fundamental categories: people, and the objects of their desires. All people are not considered equal; neither are some considered more equal than others. 'Objects of desire' are what motivate people to act in particular ways.

We start the argument by considering each person as an individual and ignoring his or her potential interactions with other people. We assume, furthermore, that each person is intrinsically motivated by 'private' desires that do not include desires about how other people ought to interact with each other. When interacting with others people will almost certainly develop 'social' desires for things such as power, prestige, reputation and glory, which make sense only when applied to social interactions, and have no meaning in relation to a single person in complete isolation from all others. We will be returning to these vitally important motivations in due course, but we will then be viewing them as *instrumental* products of social interaction rather than as *intrinsic* individual motivations.

'Rational' people are motivated by the urge to fulfil their desires. This very general definition requires more detailed specification when considered in conjunction with our first serious assumption, which is that the objects of people's desires are in short supply. This is assumed to be true even for a single isolated individual. Even Eve, the only woman in the world cannot have everything she wants. Nature sees to that. She might want to walk on water, for example, but that would be just too bad. The fulfilment of desires by an individual involves the expenditure of resources. But each individual is vested by nature with a limited stock of resources denominated, in their most basic form, in terms of physical and mental capacities such as strength, energy, endurance, determination, ingenuity and intelligence.

This means that people operate in a world which *enables* them to do certain things and *constrains* them from doing others, simultaneously offering possibilities and setting limits upon what can be achieved in certain situations. Constraints take various forms. Some are absolute and immutable – for example the amount of time available in one day. Other constraints are absolute but within the control of the individual – for example the amount of information stored in the brain. Some resources, such as time and energy, are expendable, while others, such as information and intelligence, are not. The expenditure of some resources, such as energy, is within the control of the individual; the expenditure of other resources, such as time, is not. These limits to, and constraints on, the stock of resources available for fulfilling desires mean that, for each individual, it is quite possible to have desires that cannot be fulfilled.

Some desires will be incapable of fulfilment in any circumstances. For the person concerned, these desires can be thought of as 'intrinsically' unrealizable. Thus the desires to fly unassisted or to walk on water are intrinsically unrealizable for most human beings, given the stock of resources available to them. For birds and various forms of pond life, with different stocks of resources, limitations on the fulfilment of desires will of course be different, so that unassisted flying or walking on water are matters of routine rather than hopeless aspirations.

Other desires, while not intrinsically incapable of fulfilment, cannot be fulfilled with a given stock of resources. Eve may love truffles and desire a million tons of them. While she could expend some of her resources on acquiring some truffles if she knew where to look for them, she could never accumulate a million tons of truffles in her entire lifetime (even if that many truffles exist, a delightful possibility upon which experts on the subject have sadly cast serious doubt). The desire for truffles, unlike the desire to walk on water, can be realized to some degree. Nevertheless, truffles are in short supply, since it is possible to desire more of them than can actually be found.

So far, we have considered only one desire at a time. Individuals, however, will want lots of different things. It is quite possible that a bundle of desires will contain several desires that are mutually incompatible. Either one of a pair of desires may be capable of being fulfilled on its own, but it may be impossible to fulfil both desires together. Thus, Eve may desire to have a perfect physique (body), and at the same time desire a life of indolent luxury (bed). Unwelcome but inescapable facts of nature may mean that she simply cannot fulfil both desires and must perforce choose between them. Neither object of her desires is in itself in short supply. But a bundle of desires containing both body and bed is unrealizable, because the two desires are intrinsically incompatible.

Some objects of desire that are not intrinsically incompatible may nonetheless be mutually exclusive, given the particular stock of personal resources available to the individual concerned. Eve may desire a small sack of truffles and a ton of raw steak. While she can fulfil each desire on its own, she may well not have enough time, energy, intelligence and whatever else it takes to realize both of these desires at the same time.

To sum up, fulfilling desires involves expending resources and each individual is endowed with a limited stock of resources. This constrains people by rendering some of their desires absolutely incapable, and others partially incapable, of fulfilment, and by rendering some sets of desires mutually incompatible. Only people with completely compatible sets of desires, which can all be completely fulfilled using the stock of available resources, will find that the objects of their desires are not in short supply. This book assumes that many people in the real world do not fall into this category, having desires that are incapable of complete fulfilment and therefore facing a situation in which the objects of their desires are indeed in short supply.

## Making choices

At any given moment, a person will have private desires and will confront a world that offers opportunities for, as well as constraints upon, the realization of these desires. *Actions* are available to each individual that change the world in some way. These actions have *outcomes* that have a bearing on the likelihood that particular private desires are realized. We can think of a plan for deciding which actions to take in which states of the world as a *strategy*.

A person is typically faced with choosing between several courses of action. These involve the commitment of different amounts of various types of resource and have different consequences for the fulfilment of a given bundle of desires. Faced with a choice between courses of action, a 'rational' individual in the strict sense that we will be using the term adopts a strategy that selects the course of action that most effectively fulfils his or her desires.

In order to do this Eve must be able to identify or at least estimate the *set of feasible outcomes* of each course of action that is open to her. Each of these outcomes will almost certainly have consequences for the various objects of Eve's desires. In order to identify the feasible outcome that most effectively fulfils her desires, therefore, Eve must be able to place the various objects of her desires in some sort of order of preference.[1] If Eve is faced with a choice between two courses of action, for example, one of which yields more truffles while the other yields more raw steak, she must decide which of these objects of desire she most prefers before she can decide which outcome she prefers and hence which strategy for selecting a course of action she should rationally choose.

Placing desires in an order of preference is a first step in the process of rational decision-making, but this is not sufficient to allow a rational individual to choose the best strategy in all circumstances. Since actions have consequences for *bundles of desires*, one course of action will have an expected outcome that fulfils each part of a particular bundle of desires to a certain degree. An alternative course of action may have an expected outcome that fulfils some parts of this bundle of desires more, and other parts less, than the first outcome.

If Eve, acting alone for example, places four of her objects of desire in the order bed, body, steak and truffles, then one action may generate an outcome involving lots of bed and truffles with very little body and steak. Another action may have an expected outcome involving lots of body and steak, with a shortfall in the realms of truffles and bed. Simply ranking the objects of her desires does not help Eve, in this case, to make a rational choice between the two courses of action. One course of action yields bed and truffles, her top- and bottom-ranked objects of desire, while the other action yields body and steak, her middle two preferences. Eve must decide *how much* she prefers bed to body to steak to truffles before she can make a decision. She needs, in other words, to assign *values* to her various goals before she can engage in an effective rational calculus. These values, known as 'utilities', will enable her to choose between the imperfect fulfilment of bundles of desires, when one bundle is not clearly better than the other in relation to every one of its component parts. In other words, assigning utilities will enable her to make a rational choice in the common situation in which one course of action fulfils some desires better, but others worse, than an alternative course of action.

Another circumstance in which a rational person will need to consult the utilities associated with various objects of desire is when faced with a choice between courses of action that yield *uncertain* outcomes. Ultimately, of course, every course of action that you might choose has an uncertain outcome. You may walk out of your front door on a sunny day and expect to survive the experience but it is just possible, as happened to someone a few years ago in France, that you will be killed by a giant hailstone that falls out of a clear blue sky. Strictly speaking in all cases, and as a practical necessity in most cases, we evaluate different courses of action in terms of their *probable* outcomes. Each action actually has a range of different possible outcomes, and we can assign a probability to each.

Eve in a state of nature may spot an especially juicy plum, tantalizingly out of reach at the top of a tall plum tree. She may consider climbing the tree and look hard at its branches in order to estimate whether they will bear her weight in a voyage towards the plum or dump her painfully and plumlessly on the ground. She faces a choice between two courses of action. The first is not to climb the tree, which yields the expected outcome that she remains plumless and safe on the ground (discounting as sufficiently unlikely to be not worth considering the possibility of being killed by a giant hailstone that would have missed her had she climbed the tree). The second is to climb the tree, which will yield one of two expected outcomes (discounting the possibility that the giant hailstone may take another trajectory). One possible outcome of climbing the tree is that some branch will fail to take Eve's weight and that she will end up on the ground plumless and with a broken leg. The other possible outcome of climbing the tree is that the branches will take the strain and Eve will end up on the ground both safe and in possession of the plum. Now it is fair to assume that ending up both safe and plumful is Eve's most preferred outcome, while ending up plumless and with a broken leg is seen by her as being much worse than being safe and plumless. In other words, climbing the tree may yield her top- or her bottom-ranked outcome, while staying on the ground yields her middle-ranked outcome. How does she decide what to do?

In order to calculate the expected value of keeping her feet on the ground, Eve simply has to consult her own preferences and determine the value to her of being safe and plumless, which we are taking to be an absolute certainty in this event. (In other words, the probability of this happening is estimated at 1.0.) In order to evaluate the expected value of climbing the tree, Eve must engage in a three-stage calculation. First, she must consult her preferences and determine the value to her of being (a) safe and plumful and (b) hurt and plumless. Second she must estimate the probability of these two possible outcomes. (If these are the only two possible outcomes she is considering then these probabilities must sum to one; if they do not, then either a mistake has been made or some other outcome is implicitly being envisaged.) Third, she must estimate the expected value to her of climbing the tree by adding together the value of each possible outcome, having discounted this by the probability of it actually happening. She can now compare the expected value of climbing the tree with the expected value of staying on the ground and decide what to do.

If all of this seems very unrealistic, we should note that few people actually perform such complicated calculations consciously and explicitly when contemplating more or less routine courses of action such as picking a plum. The basic premise of rational decision-making, however, is that rational people can be modelled, when they choose between the range of strategies that are open to them, as if they have made this choice on the basis of such a calculation. The issues here are very similar to those confronting us when we try to explain how people can pick their way through a crowded china shop without knocking anything over, or ride a bicycle, or sleep in a bed without falling out. The calculations involved in putting the human body in the right place at the right time are immensely complex, as anyone who has tried to design even the most simple robot will find out – too complex indeed for any normal person to perform consciously and in real time. Yet most normal people can unconsciously perform, in real time and with complete success, the complex calculations needed to perform these simple feats. The fact that the underlying calculations are so difficult does not imply that ordinary people cannot perform them.

In the terms in which we normally think about such things, when Eve is deciding whether or not to go for that plum she is deciding, probably in a barely conscious manner, whether or not the risk of falling on the ground and breaking a leg is worth the benefit of picking the plum if she survives the climb, using the safe option of keeping her feet on the ground as her baseline. People make this type of calculation many, many times every day, more or less unconsciously, and they may well not think that they are performing a rational calculus. When so doing, however, they are in practice engaging in rational behaviour by choosing the strategy that maximizes their expected utility, weighing the costs, the benefits and the risks involved.

The characterization of a rational person as a maximizer of utility is a common elaboration of the definition of a rational person as somebody who seeks to fulfil his or her desires. We can see from this example that the notion of rational choice is not at all as exotic or arcane as it might seem at first sight. To appreciate this further, imagine what it would take for a person *not* to be rational.

There are two basic ways not to be rational. The most obvious is for a person to be 'counter-rational', in the sense of consciously choosing a course of action that is known to yield a lower payoff than some alternative. For example, Eve may hate both plums and broken legs, and know that she will almost certainly fall out of the tree and break a leg if she tries to pick the plum, but may nonetheless climb the tree and fall out of it rather than stay safe on the ground. It would be hard to describe her behaviour as rational in such circumstances. If chosen in the knowledge of the payoff and the probabilities, it would be counter-rational.

Another way not to be rational is wantonly to refuse to evaluate the potential outcomes before making a decision. Imagine, for example, that Eve sees a whole sack of truffles on an island surrounded by water that is much deeper than Eve is tall. Eve spots the truffles from the shore and, without thinking any more about it, begins to make her way to the island, omitting to consider the fact that she cannot swim. Sad to say, she drowns. Her behaviour is not really counter-rational in the sense that she did not explicitly choose a bad course of action; rather she failed to evaluate a course of action when it would have been both extremely easy to do this, and very easy to see that her choice was a most damaging one. 'Stupid' is a word that springs immediately to mind to describe this behaviour, but it is perhaps characterized in a more neutral way as 'reckless'. Reckless behaviour is non-rational in the sense that, in circumstances when it would have been very easy to calculate which was the best course of action, the individual concerned simply did not make this calculation.

The notion of reckless behaviour draws our attention to the fact that the process of actually evaluating the outcomes of actions may well in itself be costly. The costs involved may include time consumed in making the assessment, all sort of costs involved in gathering the necessary information, together with the mental energy and other resources expended in actually identifying the most fruitful course of action. These costs are very important, since it may just not be cost-effective to evaluate certain courses of action if the costs of doing this outweigh the *prima facie* benefits of making the correct choice.

If the sack of truffles is sitting on an island surrounded by deep and freezing cold water covered in thin ice, for example, much time, thought and energy might be expended by Eve in order to decide upon her best route to the sack, since the costs of choosing the wrong route and ending up under the ice in the freezing water would be huge. A person who proceeded very cautiously indeed across the ice, calculating every step with the utmost precision, would clearly, and rightly, be seen as quite rational. If the same sack of truffles is sitting in the middle of a dry grassy meadow, on a bed of beautiful and sweet-smelling wild flowers, it may still be true that one route to the truffles is likely to be better than another if we measure the time taken to get to the sack in microseconds. Most routes will be so similar, however, that any costs incurred in deciding upon the very best route would almost certainly be wasted. Indeed (assuming that there was not the slightest reason to suspect that the grassy meadow was littered with vicious anti-personnel mines) a person who proceeded very cautiously indeed across the meadow, calculating every step with utmost precision, would clearly, and rightly, be seen as quite mad.

The difference between the two cases is that there is a strong *prima facie* case for arguing that the precise route across the thin ice makes a very big difference, and needs to be chosen with great care, while the precise route across the grassy meadow, while possibly making a very tiny difference, can hardly make so much of a difference that it is worth spending any resources to identify the best route. Thus the person who walks 'boldly' out on the thin ice without the slightest regard to which route to take is just plain reckless, and in this sense non-rational, even if by some chance the truffles are collected and the shore is regained without accident. In contrast the person who walks boldly across the meadow and picks up the sack of truffles is being quite rational, despite doing this in the knowledge that there might just be a route to the truffles that would have taken a microsecond less to traverse. To spend more than a microsecond finding this route would clearly be counter-productive.

This rational decision-making must take account of the cost of making a rational decision, as well as the benefits that might arise from this – a judgement that must be made on the basis of the *prima facie* evidence at the disposal of the decision-maker. Not to expend any resources on a decision when the *prima facie* evidence is that there is no difference between courses of action is a quite rational response to the fact that decisions themselves involve costs. Not to expend resources on a decision when the *prima facie* evidence is that there is a big difference between courses of action is what we have called reckless behaviour, and it is clearly, in our terms, non-rational. It may of course turn out that the grassy meadow is in fact a minefield and our rational decision-maker is quite unexpectedly blown to a thousand pieces *en route* to the truffles. This would be bad luck rather than recklessness, however, the sort of thing that not only Eve but also most economists and rational choice theorists would refer to as a *shock*, if there was not even the slightest reason to suspect the possibility of mines before the voyage across the field was undertaken.

In the long term reckless behaviour is also counter-rational since it is almost certain that a large number of actions chosen recklessly will yield a lower payoff than a large number of actions chosen rationally. In relation to a particular choice, however, it may be helpful to make a distinction between reckless and counter-rational behaviour.

Decision-making that is neither reckless nor counter-rational is rational. In effect, to claim that people do not typically behave rationally is to claim that they typically behave either counter-rationally or recklessly, which in my humble submission is a far more bizarre and far-fetched claim. Of course people may make *imperfect* rational decisions, if they have bad and incomplete information or make mistakes when calculating expected utilities, but this is quite another matter. And people may take calculated risks that do not pay off, climbing the plum tree in search of a lusted-after plum and being dumped painfully on the ground, for example. Taking calculated risks is part of the very essence of rational decision-making, however, which certainly does not imply that risk-takers are always paid off with the good rather than the bad consequences of the risks that they take.

## Instrumental desires

Thus far we have considered only those objects of desire that people value 'intrinsically', things that are valued *for their own sake*. We now assume that individuals may also desire things that are not valued in themselves, but rather because they can help to achieve things that are intrinsically valued. For example if Eve is thirsty, she can lie on her back with her mouth wide open when it rains. This will not be a very efficient way of quenching her thirst. She may decide that some form of water-collector, such as a bucket, will gather much more rainwater in much less time. This will leave her not only with more to drink, but with more time available to her to fulfil other desires. She will value the bucket, not because she has any intrinsic desire to possess a bucket as such, but because it helps her to fulfil other of her intrinsic desires. We can think of things such as buckets that are valued only because they help to fulfil other desires as being 'instrumentally' valued. The analytical classification of the objects of desire into those that are instrumentally and those that are intrinsically valued is, of course, simply a definitional exercise. In practice, many objects of desire will have both intrinsic and instrumental value. Eve may value good health, for example, because it enables her to fulfil all sorts of other desires, as well as because she derives intrinsic satisfaction simply from being healthy.

To summarize, we have been concerned up until now with a socially isolated rational individual who tries to fulfil desires for things that are effectively in short supply. This involves placing goals in an order of preference and, usually, assigning more precise values to them. These utilities will facilitate decisions between risky courses of action, and between outcomes fulfilling bundles of different desires to different degrees. Some objects of desire will be intrinsically valued; others will be valued mainly because they are instrumental to the fulfilment of more intrinsically motivated desires.

## More people

We have so far considered the behaviour of each rational inhabitant of our universe as if no one else existed. Now consider a universe populated by more than one rational person, opening up the possibility that some will be able to fulfil their desires while others will not. Things that are not in short supply with respect to a single individual may be in short supply if they are desired by a group of individuals. Furthermore, there may be things that are in short supply even for individuals but which are in even shorter supply when desired by a group of individuals. In these circumstances, people will find themselves in a state of potential competition with each other over the fulfilment of their desires.

It is clear that this competition will not only concern intrinsically valued objects of desire, but will also extend to the instrumental means to realize these. A direct consequence of such competition is that people may seek to prevent others from fulfilling desires for things that they themselves want. Furthermore they may be able to realize the objects of their desires by expropriating these from other people, rather than by expropriating them directly from their physical environment. This potential competition between individuals therefore provides a justification for important new types of instrumental objective. These will be tools for resisting encroachment from others, tools for preventing others from fulfilling desires that conflict or compete with those of others, and tools for expropriating objects of desire from others rather than directly from nature.

These instrumental means of attack and defence can be thought of as weapons. Weapons can be both physical and psychological. The physical value of an enormous spiky club is obvious. Consider, however, an individual who had destroyed all previous opponents with an enormous spiky club. The successful and ruthless use of this physical weapon over a period of time will create certain expectations on the part of potential competitors and likely victims, perhaps discouraging them from going anywhere near the club-wielder. It may even become unnecessary to wield the club at all, as potential competitors flee when a beclubbed silhouette looms on the horizon. A *reputation* for wielding the club would thus achieve the same effect as the club itself. This reputation would be a sort of psychological weapon, valued instrumentally since it would greatly assist the owner in fulfilling all sorts of other desires. An individual could develop such a reputation by going around clubbing all and sundry, whether or not they were likely to be rivals, simply in order to become known as a hard case.

One of the interesting things about a reputation, apart from the fact that rational choice theorists have become increasingly interested in the role of reputations in recent years, is that it can take a very long time to build a reputation that can be effectively destroyed in seconds. A reputation for utter ruthlessness with the spiky club, for example, may be built painstakingly, even painfully, over the years on the basis of the relentless repetition of ruthless acts. A reputation for honourable behaviour may take years of honourable behaviour to develop. But a single act of pointless mercy when utter ruthlessness was expected, a single dastardly deed when 'doing the right thing' was anticipated, can destroy these carefully crafted reputations at a stroke. Such reputations, viewed in these terms, represent huge but very fragile instrumental investments for the people who own them.

In the argument that follows, we will often focus on the role of an individual's reputation in helping him or her to achieve specific objectives.

Since a person's reputation can be very useful in many different situations, it is a very valuable *socially defined* asset that can be developed when somebody interacts over a period of time with the same group of fellow human beings, and when these interactions are observed, interpreted and remembered by others. This means that somebody may well develop and protect a reputation – paying debts when it would be more profitable, narrowly construed, to renege on these, for example – rather than acting to fulfil short-term private desires.

At this point it is important to re-emphasize one of the major implications of the methodological style of the argument in this book, discussed in the previous chapter. We are setting out to construct a fundamental potential explanation of the political world, and therefore must be careful to ensure that the motivational assumptions we make about individuals do not include intrinsic desires concerning how other people should interact with each other. Rational people in groups will develop all sorts of desires that are 'socially defined', in the sense that these do deal with interactions between other people. The use of fundamental potential explanations demands that we make the crucial assumption that these socially defined motivations yield no intrinsic value for the individual and are felt solely for instrumental reasons.

This critical assumption is the engine that gives us intellectual lift-off, and provides the distinctive character of rational choice theory. The statement that a rational individual is a maximizer of utility is insufficient in itself to achieve this, if we allow utility to be derived from absolutely anything. If any action can be rational, because there will always be some desire that it fulfils, then our core assumptions are insufficiently constrained to generate more than truisms. We can always dream up somebody who desires just the right type of social interactions to solve any problem we might encounter. Eliminating the possibility of intrinsic desires for particular types of social interaction and requiring that such desires be instrumentally justified provides a very strong constraint and hence considerable analytical purchase. It is this, rather than any statement about utility-maximization, that allows us to make non-trivial deductions about the political world. The point of the whole endeavour is to take certain important types of political interaction and construct fundamental potential explanations of these. Rational choice theories that do not employ these, or equivalent, constraints are doomed to triviality.

I should stress at this point that what I have been presenting is very much the rational choice theorists' view of rationality. Nozick (1993) shows us quite clearly that this is certainly not the only possible view of the matter. He develops a description of a more broadly conceived rational calculus, encompassing the possibility that rational people may hedge their bets between various different personal decision-making procedures that might appeal to them, and do so in different ways in different social and political contexts.

Once we think about the social context of rational decision-making, it is important to distinguish two rather different ways in which the typical highly simplified model of a rational decision might be challenged. One way is to note that any description of a particular decision problem must be stylized in order to make it tractable theoretically, that something is lost in the stylization, and that a more realistic description of the same problem is almost certain to reveal incentives and motivations not evident in the stylized version. Thus if I borrow money from you and am trying to decide whether to pay it back or not, we clearly lose something if we ignore the fact that I might want to borrow more money from you in the future; or that others with whom I may need to deal some day will find out what has happened; or that I will personally feel bad if I do not honour a promise that I make. Broadening the context will, of course, change the analysis of this interaction.

To identify aspects of a decision problem that a particular group of rational choice theorists have inadvertently overlooked, or which they have consciously chosen not to take into account, is not to criticize rational choice theory as a whole. But the need to generate a theoretically tractable stylized description of the world does present us with an inescapable problem. This arises not only from the need to ignore things in the interests of simplification, but also from the fact that what, precisely, is ignored may make a rational act appear to be irrational, or vice versa. All of this is a problem for theory in general, and not for rational choice theory in particular – in a sense a theory is not a theory at all if it addresses itself to every conceivable detail of every case. We should therefore distinguish between limited applications of rational choice theory, on the one hand, and the analytical potential of the approach when we look at a decision problem in its broadest *practicable* context, on the other. As rational choice theory has developed, it has indeed become more sophisticated in its view of the ways in which an interaction under study is embedded in a network of other interactions, each with a bearing upon the other. The problems that remain are typically those of analytical tractability – even highly simplified specifications of a problem can be very, very difficult to analyse – rather than of some failure of imagination on the part of the theorists involved.

The second type of challenge to the type of rational calculus that I have described does represent a fundamental difference of opinion about how decisions are made. Despite all of the added complexity and refinement that might be gained by looking at ever more realistic social and political contexts of a given decision, the fundamental decision-maker remains an individual human being. The real bottom line is that there are individual actions, that there are outcomes of these actions, and that *individuals choose actions in terms of their outcomes*, using some decision rule or another. This is the heart of rational choice theory, and it does not admit of the possibility that groups of individuals choose actions in some way that is fundamentally more than an interactive product, however complex, of the choices of individual members of the group.

This does not mean that rational choice theorists assume that the decisions of a group of people are the simple sum of the decisions of each member of the group. But it does mean, and we should make no bones about this, that the decision of a group of people can in some way be inferred from the decision of each group member – that there is not some extra added ingredient in the decision that depends upon the group having a collective mind over and above the individual minds of its members. This is ultimately why rational choice theory is seen as being essentially individualistic, and rightly so. Once we talk about a group making decisions in a way that cannot be adduced in some way, however byzantine, from the collected decisions of group members, then we are moving outside the rational choice approach.

This imposes a surprisingly rigid intellectual discipline on the arguments we make. When you read the general things that people write about politics, it really is quite remarkable how often people write about groups of people, organizations, political parties and many other quintessentially social institutions in strongly anthropomorphic terms. We often hear, for example, that 'the party decided to change its leader', or that 'the army staged a coup d'état', 'the trade union decided to take on the management' as if these social entities in some way had minds of their own. Rarely does the author of such statements suggest how, in practice, this collective mind might work. Perhaps rational choice theory's greatest single virtue is that it does force us to think hard about this.

## The social context of private desires

Any individual who must coexist with others will quickly become aware of the distinctive social context of many objects of intrinsic private desire. Two central aspects of this social context concern the realization, or production, of objects of desire and their enjoyment, or consumption. The social context of production arises from the inescapable fact that individuals may well desire things that no individual is capable of producing single-handed – so that the process of realizing private desires is inherently collective. The social context of consumption arises from the (also inescapable) fact that, when one individual consumes a good, this typically has a bearing upon the consumption of this and other goods by other people.

### The social context of consumption

For no better reason than to polish my prose, I shall in what follows often refer to objects of desire as 'goods'. In doing this I am thinking of goods in a very general way, to comprise not only the goods and services that economists and shopkeepers like so much to talk about, but also anything else that might be an object of desire and hence motivate people to act.

We can think of some goods as being very 'private' in the manner of their enjoyment or consumption. When I consume a 'private' good such as this, I personally appropriate the whole of the benefit of that good. An excellent example of a private consumption good is a piece of food, such as a banana, that I might pluck from its natural state, hanging on a banana tree, and eat. My consumption of a particular banana makes it considerably less attractive (as a banana) to others. Even in this example, of course, the banana may be the one piece of food that keeps me alive when I am on the point of dying of starvation, and I may go on to discover a way of preventing people from developing cancer. The consumption of the apparently private banana may thus have massive public significance. But the fact does remain that, once I have eaten it, the object that I saw, desired and then plucked from a tree ceases to be what most normal people understand to be a 'banana'. The banana itself has now become part of me while its skin, should I carelessly toss this on the path, becomes a hazard for unwary pedestrians.

The polar opposite of a private consumption good is a public consumption good. Imagine that I did indeed find a simple way in which people could change their lifestyle and thereby avoid developing cancer, and that as a result cancer was eradicated from the face of the earth. This would be of truly momentous significance for a very large proportion of the world's population. It would affect not only those who have cancer now and those who would otherwise have cancer in the future. It would also affect those who would never, in fact, have contracted cancer, but who fear contracting it, and whose lives are made more miserable by that fear.

Crucially in this context, the benefits to me of avoiding cancer in no way whatsoever impinge upon you – cancer is not somehow less absent once I have personally enjoyed its absence. Quite unlike a banana, I can't 'use up' the eradication of cancer. The entire world could enjoy this and there would still be just as much of it as there was at the beginning. For infectious diseases, indeed, I am made better off when you are cured – far from using up the cure when you are cured, you add to it! This type of object of desire is sometimes referred to as a *public good*, 'which all enjoy in common in the sense that each individual's consumption of such a good leads to no subtraction from any other individual's consumption of that good' (Samuelson, 1954: 387).

In fact, once we start to think a little harder about the distinction between 'public' and 'private' goods, we see that this is multi-faceted. There are various features of any given good that affect the extent to which it is collectively consumed. Among these are the 'jointness or divisibility of supply', the 'excludability', the 'optionality' and the 'susceptibility to crowding' exhibited by the good in question. 'Jointness of supply' and 'excludability' form part of Samuelson's (1954) original definition of a public good, although he saw these properties as being discrete rather than continuous. 'Optionality' and 'crowding' were first discussed, among others, by Riker and Ordeshook (1973).

*Crowding*   We have defined a private good as one for which all of the utility arising from consumption goes to one person, 'the consumer'. Obviously, this person then 'crowds' all the others out of potential consumption of the good. I eat the banana, there is no banana left for anyone else. In the case of a cure for cancer, enjoyment by one person does not result in any less enjoyment of the cure by others. Indeed any number of people can enjoy the cure for cancer, and they use it up no more than if no one at all enjoyed it. The cure for cancer is thus not susceptible to crowding. Other goods will not be purely private, but will be susceptible to some crowding. A park, for example, can be used by a fair number of people with no subtraction from the enjoyment of others (except the most miserable misanthropes who hate to see anyone else in the park). There will come a point, however, when the addition of more people reduces the enjoyment of others, because the park is becoming too crowded for the tastes of most of those who are in it. Obviously, very small parks might be quite susceptible to crowding, but they are clearly not private goods like bananas. A fantastically large park, one the size of the Sahara Desert, may be hardly susceptible at all to crowding. The less susceptible to crowding a good is, the more public it is, because the less use by one consumer restricts its use by others.

*Optionality*  We have so far been thinking in terms of people having particular objects of desire and making choices designed to help them fulfil these. While in some cases a person does have a choice about whether to consume the good in question or not, in other cases goods are forced upon people without regard to their actions or desires. Thus people may choose whether or not to eat a banana or take a walk in a park, but they cannot choose whether or not to consume a nuclear missile. Once this missile is pointed and fired at them, they will consume it (or rather it will consume *them*) whether they want to or not. The difference between a banana and a nuclear missile makes it clear that the more optional a 'good' is, the more private it is, since the smaller the probability that somebody will be forced to consume something against their will. The less optional a good is, the more public.

The degree of 'optionality' may be measured in terms of the costs to an individual of opting out of consuming the good in question. It costs you nothing to opt out of consuming a park, unless you happen to live in the middle of it; just don't go there. But it costs an enormous amount to opt out of a nuclear missile pointed in your direction. Opting out of the loud and tasteless music spilling out of your neighbour's birthday party may involve some modest cost to you as you make your own loud but tasteful music to drown out the din, or give up and go out to the pub.

*Excludability*  If consumption of a good is absolutely non-optional, then it is obviously impossible to exclude specified people from consuming it. Thus I can't really point a nuclear missile at you and exclude your neighbours from its effects. If a good is optional, however, it might or might not be possible to make a conscious decision to exclude others from it. It is very easy to exclude people from a park, for example, but almost impossible to exclude them from a beautiful sunset, despite the fact that the enjoyment of both is entirely optional. If cost is no object, of course, it is possible to exclude almost anyone from almost anything. I could build enormous screens to exclude you from some beautiful sunset, for example, but these would be very expensive. While people might pay me to see the sunset if I could control access to it, they would probably never pay me enough to cover the cost of building the screens and gaining that control. The exclusion of people from some good may thus have greater costs than can be recouped as a direct consequence of being able to control access to it. Thus sunsets are effectively not excludable, while parks are, since it is easy to put gates or guards around a park, and likely that people would pay a high enough entry fee for these costs to be recovered. Indeed, if I install exciting rides, magic castles and other entertaining paraphernalia in my park, you might even pay quite a lot for the privilege of being allowed, with your family, to use the park for a day. It would then pay me to build quite a high fence around my park, and hire fierce guards to discourage those bent upon enjoying the park without paying. The degree of 'excludability' of any object of desire is thus measured in terms of the cost of exclusion relative to the potential benefits. Goods will tend to be excludable or not in a given context, depending upon whether or not exclusion costs can be recouped.

*Jointness of supply*   A jointly supplied good is one that, if it is available for consumption at all by any members of a group, is available for consumption in equal measure by all members of the group. (Note that membership of the group of consumers may be flexible if the good is excludable.) A purely private good is perfectly divisible, and can thus be supplied in any mix of quantities to any mix of people. A jointly supplied good must be made available in the same quantity to all consumers. A small park is a thus jointly supplied good, despite the fact that it is susceptible to crowding, while a cure for cancer is a jointly supplied good which cannot be crowded. A nuclear missile, however, may be consumed in different measure by different inhabitants of an island. People living near the point where the missile lands will consume an awful lot of it; depending on the power of the missile, people living hundreds of miles away from the point of impact will consume rather less. Thus, a nuclear missile is not necessarily jointly supplied, although it is a very public sort of 'good' in many other respects, being non-optional, non-crowdable and non-excludable.

## The social context of production

Many desires can be fulfilled by an individual acting in total isolation from all others. These include, for example, the gathering of nuts and berries and the provision of rudimentary shelter. At the opposite extreme, there are objects of desire that can only be realized by large groups of people acting in concert, even if each individual possesses huge resources. A concert, indeed, is a very good example of such a good. Compared to the joy of listening to 50 musicians playing simultaneously in perfect harmony, one person running around playing each instrument in turn is not at all the same thing. Catching a magnificent wild elephant alive would be another excellent example of something that is certainly much easier for mere mortals to achieve as a team of people acting together than as single people acting in isolation. Such desires require 'joint production' if they are ever to be realized at all.

Between these extremes lies a wide range of goods which can, in principle at least, be produced by an isolated individual, but can be much more efficiently and economically produced when individuals act in concert. Thus, while an isolated Robinson Crusoe might trap a smallish wild animal on his own, a possum perhaps, organized bands of hunters can realize vast increases in productivity, encircling entire herds of over-excited wild elephants. Thus in addition to private desires that simply cannot be fulfilled by an isolated individual, there are those subject to economies of scale, gains from trade, division of labour and other forms of social activity.

*Production, consumption and technology*

Publicness of consumption and publicness of production are not so much 'intrinsic' properties of a given good as features of a certain level of technology. The radio broadcasting frequency spectrum is a good example of this. Back in the old days of steam radio, when broadcasting equipment was complex and expensive, relatively few people had the ability to broadcast. The problem of crowding by too many broadcasters using similar frequencies, and of the resulting interference between them and general degradation of the resource, was not great. It was also easy enough to track down broadcasters and stop them from broadcasting, if necessary by throwing them in jail and confiscating their equipment. The broadcasting frequency spectrum was like a large public park in a lightly settled area. As ever more broadcasters wanted to use the resource and as the cost of broadcasting declined precipitously, the broadcasting frequency spectrum became crowded. It was as if the same public park had been moved into the heart of a major city. As broadcasting technology improved, two things happened. The effective carrying capacity of the frequency spectrum was vastly increased by more efficient broadcasting equipment and techniques, while broadcasting technology itself became cheaper and cheaper – so cheap in fact that almost anyone who wants to broadcast can do so. Detection and elimination of all rogue broadcasters thereby became more or less impossible.

This is not the place to elaborate on the very interesting politics of the broadcasting frequency spectrum, but the impact of technology on the social context of broadcasting does serve to make the point that what might superficially seem to be the 'publicness' or 'privateness' of a good is very much technologically determined, and hence subject to change over time as technology develops.

*The interaction of production and consumption*

The publicness of consumption and of production of a given good combine to generate a range of different political interactions. A *public, or collective consumption, good* that can be efficiently *produced on a purely private basis* presents no real problems in this regard. As long as the production of the good yields a private surplus to the person producing it, then rational people will produce it, despite the fact that the benefits of this can be enjoyed by others. Thus someone who enjoys making beautiful music may go ahead and make music despite the 'free' benefits to others who are able to hear it. Such musicians might wish that they could charge others for these benefits but, if the music cannot economically be withheld from non-payers, then musicians will not stop playing just to spite those who enjoy the fruits of their artistry for nothing.

Public benefits to others that arise from the fulfilment of private desires by individuals are typically referred to as spillovers, externalities or external effects. In the case of an accomplished musician playing beautiful music, the external effects are positive, so that others enjoy something that they see as a benefit without personal cost. In the case of an enthusiastic but essentially untalented young child just starting to play the trumpet, however, the externalities may be extremely painful for all others within earshot, save possibly the most doting of parents. Generically, we can think of negative externalities as 'pollution' since almost all of these, for example the deadly fumes pumping relentlessly out of my car's exhaust pipe when I drive through a beautiful landscape, tend to appear as costs paid by innocent bystanders.

Many *privately consumed* goods, however, can only be *produced collectively*. Indeed when we consider bundles of different private consumption goods, as opposed to the individual goods on their own, then gains arising from joint production will almost always be obvious. Groups of people, each endowed with different amounts of different types of resource, each facing different environmental constraints, and each having different private desires, will almost invariably find that they can realize gains from trading with one another. I have something you want. You have something I want. We're both better off if we trade these things. Trade is one means of co-ordinating the collective fulfilment of bundles of private desires, taking advantage of efficient divisions of labour, or economies of scale.

The most serious political problems tend to arise over the *collective production* of goods that are also *collectively consumed*. Consider a group of people locked in a small room. All are pathological smokers but each is aware that, if they all smoke at the same time, the air will quickly become unbreathable and they might even die from asphyxiation. The air in the room is equally available to all, none can be excluded from it, so it is non-optional. (This excludes the ridiculous situation in which each person in the room goes about in a private oxygen tent.) Even though the room's air can become crowded, in the sense that one person breathing the air does leave a little less oxygen for others, the air is to a great extent collectively consumed by all who are in the room. Having breathable air in the room depends upon there being at most a few people who are smoking. This is therefore a collectively produced good, since no individual acting alone (without a machine-gun) can produce it. If the smokers are relatively depraved nicotine addicts, so that none can really tell the difference in the air when one person more, or one person less, smokes in the room, then a roomful of breathable air will be very difficult to produce. Each addict will want to reap the benefits of breathable air without contributing to the costs of this by not smoking and suffering the pain of nicotine withdrawal. There will consequently be a grave risk of asphyxiation and disaster.

Similarly, we have already seen how rational people will desire weapons of offence and defence. Yet the investment of resources in weapons is not an intrinsically productive activity. Such resources are wasted in the sense that, if no weapons existed, then people would be able instead to devote their resources exclusively to fulfilling their intrinsic desires. The group as a whole would be much better off if all members agreed to disarm. Any individual member of the group would be better off, however, allowing the others to disarm, then appearing with an enormous spiky club and simply stealing the objects of her desires from others. It is unlikely that anyone in the group would expose themselves to this risk, so that they will all be forced to continue spending scarce resources on weapons. This is because group disarmament is both a collective consumption good and a collective production good. All can enjoy some of the benefits of disarmament, whether they disarm or not, yet disarmament cannot be achieved at all unless a number of people co-operate. The collective security brought about by unanimous multilateral disarmament is an excellent example of a good requiring joint production, since it is impossible to produce it at all without the participation of every member of the group. It will be more common, however, for goods to be jointly produced, not because all of the group must participate in production, but because the investments involved would not be cost-effective for a single individual.

Thus, a group of sailors may each want a lighthouse, but no single sailor would profit from it if she had to pay for the whole lighthouse single-handed. In such cases, a person's participation in the production process will often amount to nothing more elevated than a contribution to the costs of production. Often, any particular individual contribution will not be at all critical to the production of the good in question, so that the expected value of consuming the good is, for a single consumer, quite unrelated to any contributions that he or she might make.

Our group of rational people would have to be quite large, for them to contemplate building themselves a lighthouse. Any sailor in this large group would know that her contribution would almost certainly make no perceivable difference to the value of the lighthouse. The light will shine just as brightly with or without it. Since the lighthouse can of its nature be enjoyed by all and sundry, whether or not those who enjoy it have also contributed to the cost of production, rational sailors will not contribute. The consequence is that this brightly shining navigational aid will not be built, despite the fact that it is desired by all.

This is the 'collective action problem'. It arises when rational people desire collective consumption goods from which they cannot economically be excluded, and when each individual's contribution to the production of these yields a directly consequential benefit that is less than the cost involved. Rational individuals will then have strong incentives to enjoy the benefits of the good without paying for it, and in this sense to take 'free rides' on it. (It is for this reason that the problem is also often referred to as the 'free rider' problem.) Since many people may have incentives to take free rides on goods from which they cannot be excluded, it may be impossible actually to produce such goods at all. All will thereby be made worse off as a result of the loss of a good that they value – a good that they would indeed have been prepared to pay for if they could somehow have been excluded from consuming it when they failed to pay.

Since utterly non-excludable goods are something of an abstraction, rarely met in reality, it might be argued that the collective action problem can for the most part be solved by finding ways of excluding from the consumption of a good those who do not participate in producing it. Exclusion is often a costly process, however, represents a public good to the group of existing contributors, and must be financed from somewhere. Furthermore, if excluding recalcitrants costs resources, it is quite possible that the benefits obtained (in terms of the increased likelihood of contributions) are less than the cost.

This cost-benefit calculation will, of course, have an important strategic dimension. It may be worth excluding some free riders at a loss, in order to prevent others from getting funny ideas about not paying. Whatever the results of these strategic calculations, it will be difficult under our core assumptions to provide mechanisms for excluding free riders, precisely because such exclusion mechanisms are themselves public goods subject to free-riding. Many goods may therefore become effective collective consumption goods because of the problem of providing exclusion mechanisms.

Thus objects of desire can be either privately or collectively consumed, and either privately or collectively produced. Polar examples of each type of good include bananas, which can be privately plucked from nature and consumed, and sophisticated consumer goods such as personal compact disc players, which can be privately consumed but require very complex joint production. A lifestyle change that eliminates cancer is likely to be collectively produced and will be collectively consumed. Finally, technical innovation or high art are often privately produced, but publicly consumed.

This is summarized in Figure 2.1, which looks at polar extremes of the social context of production and consumption and ignores the fact that many goods may in practice lie somewhere in between these extremes.

CONSUMPTION

|  | Collective | Private |
|---|---|---|
| **Collective** | Absence of cancer | Compact disc player |
| PRODUCTION | | |
| **Private** | Art | Banana |

Figure 2.1 *Examples of collectively consumed, and collectively produced, objects of desire*

At least one collective consumption good will be an instrumentally essential precursor to the fulfilment of private desires in any social environment. This is a system that leads to the honouring of agreements between individuals. Wherever there are gains from trade, rational individuals will want to make trading agreements with one another. The scope of these agreements will be drastically reduced if they are limited to those that must be consummated instantly by handing somebody one side of the bargain with one hand, while at the same time taking the other side of the bargain with the other hand. A transaction involving a *future* commitment can be effected only if those involved anticipate that the commitment will be honoured. There must therefore be some chance that future commitments will be honoured before many deals of potentially great mutual value can be made. A system that leads to the honouring of commitments, by whatever means, would be a very valuable collective consumption good in itself, since the gains from trade that result are potentially available to all.

This means that there will be at least some collectively produced and collectively consumed goods that will be desired by rational individuals under our core assumptions. The remainder of this book will be to a large extent concerned with various potential solutions to the problem of how to fulfil private desires for these.

## Note

1. From now on, since I will only ever consider feasible outcomes, I will drop the adjective 'feasible'.

# 3

# Collective Action

We have just seen that a key political problem confronting rational people is that they may well desire things that no individual person can possibly provide in isolation from all others. Satisfying private desires is almost certain to require collective action of some sort. When an individual can be excluded from enjoying the benefits of a good that is collectively produced, then he or she has an incentive to contribute to its production. When no such exclusion is possible, a rational individual faces a strong incentive to take free rides. It may well be that so many people will take free rides that insufficient resources are available for good to be produced, making all who value the good, including the free riders, worse off. This is the collective action problem, frequently associated in the political science literature with Mancur Olson's book, *The Logic of Collective Action* (1965).

In one circumstance the collective action problem will solve itself. If production of a particular good requires the unanimous co-operation of a particular group of people, then the refusal of any single individual to co-operate will result in the good not being produced. If the good is valued by each member of the group more than the costs of his or her contribution to its production, then it will not be rational for any group member to opt out. Such goods will therefore be produced, despite the fact that they are collectively consumed.

Examples of this type of good are rather hard to come by but some do exist. Imagine that the group of addicted smokers we berated in the previous chapter now find themselves in a locked room in which they suspect there is a gas leak. Not being blown up in a major gas explosion is regarded by each of them as a good thing, something that requires the co-operation of the entire group. Each individual addicted smoker would dearly love, other things being equal, to light up a cigarette, but each knows that, in order to produce the desirable state of unblownupness, every single group member must contribute by not lighting up. Provided that none is feeling both suicidal and misanthropic, every group member finds it quite easy to come to the decision not to strike a light in the room filled with gas. The absence of global thermonuclear war may well be attributable to a similar logic. In general, since the collective action problem arises because each rational individual can take free rides that do not in themselves jeopardize production of the good, it will not apply to goods that require unanimous co-operation if they are to be produced at all.

In practice, however, we come across many, many examples of goods that require some, but not total, co-operation between group members if they are to be produced, and which people can enjoy whether or not they have contributed to the costs of production. It is these goods that are susceptible to the collective action problem. Generic real world examples of goods of this type involve the absence of many forms of pollution. A single person burning smoky fuel in a domestic hearth, for example, does not really create very much of a problem for the environment, but an entire city full of people doing precisely the same thing can create a dangerous level of smog that is not at all what these people want and may even kill some of those burning the fires. Yet once the smog has become a reality no one person can make much of a difference to it. The 'bad' of smog is collectively produced. Eradicating smog requires collective effort, in which no single individual's role is critical. Every inhabitant of the city, privately enjoying the comfort of a nice warm fire, will want to avoid giving this up as a personal contribution to the collective cost of smog reduction. Whether or not one person does light that fire and take a free ride on the atmosphere makes no real difference in itself to the level of smog. Such free riding is thus quite rational. If everybody takes individually rational free rides in this way, however, so as to enjoy the benefits of a nice warm fire in the comfort of their own home, then all of them will be afflicted by smog, and thereby be made individually worse off than they would be in the smog-free world that it is in their collective power to create. Goods of this type, and there are many of them, are susceptible to the collective action problem

Olson himself suggests a number of solutions to the collective action problem. The first is to find some way of excluding free riders. If this is possible it will obviously do the trick, assuming that such exclusion is cost-effective. There are many types of collective consumption good that it may be technologically and economically feasible to provide in this way. Lighthouses can be transformed into radio beacons operating on scrambled frequencies decoded only on payment of a fee, television broadcasts can be similarly scrambled, access to 'public' roads can be offered only to those who pay a fee for 'smart cards', and so on. In a sense, however, 'privatizing' collective consumption goods in this way does not get to the heart of the 'real' collective action problem. Given that such goods can indeed be privatized, the decision not to do so and to allow the possibility of free riding is a political choice rather than a fundamental matter of social organization.

Some goods, however, cannot be physically produced in this manner, at least at current levels of technology. Examples include clean air and collective security. Additionally, as we saw in the previous chapter, it may be very expensive to develop and produce goods in such a way as to allow free riders to be excluded. Examples include public art and architecture. Quite apart from detracting from the architecture itself, it would not be cost-effective to erect screens around public buildings, forcing those who wished to enjoy the beautiful architecture to pay a fee to enter the space from which the building could be viewed. In short, for technical and/or economic reasons, many collective consumption goods cannot feasibly be 'privatized'. Alternative methods of provision must clearly be sought if contributions to production costs cannot be enforced and free riders cannot be excluded from the pleasures of consumption.

The second method suggested by Olson for overcoming the collective action problem is for groups to provide exclusive private benefits as incentives to contributing members, in exchange for contributions to the costs of producing goods from which free riders cannot be excluded. These private benefits must be cheap enough to produce for the surplus generated from contributions to be large enough to provide both the collective consumption good and the private benefits that are offered as inducements.

It must immediately be noted that our core assumptions do not include the possibility that groups of individuals will *intrinsically* value producing collective consumption goods *per se*. Indeed our core assumptions explicitly preclude this possibility in their statement that socially defined objectives must be instrumentally valued. It is at this juncture that we see quite clearly one of the analytical benefits of insisting on fundamental potential explanations that map statements about the individual sphere on to statements about the social world. If we were not rigorous in this matter, then we would be allowed to imagine people (secular saints, in effect) who did indeed derive positive intrinsic pleasure from producing collective consumption goods. The collective action problem would then be solved at a stroke. All that would be needed would be to locate some saints and put them in charge of producing collective goods. The more that were produced, the happier the saints would be, and the happier all the free riders would be too. The only remaining problem would be to prevent people from collapsing from perpetual orgasms of happiness, though of course this problem could be solved by assuming that our saints only derive pleasure from producing *just the right amount* of collective consumption goods! This would be the political equivalent of a perpetual motion machine but would not, in any real sense, get us anywhere.

In the absence of secular saints we cannot automatically assume that, if some rational producer derives a surplus from the provision of private incentives to some group, then the producer will voluntarily and altruistically devote this surplus to the provision of collective consumption goods to group members. Olson does implicitly make this assumption, however. His example of a trade union selling insurance to workers in order to induce them to join the union, and thereby contribute to collective bargaining benefits for fellow workers that can be enjoyed regardless of union membership, illustrates this point. When it sells insurance, the trade union is an insurance broker engaged in private transactions. If these private transactions provide union members with sufficient private surplus to justify joining, then they will join anyway, whether or not a collective good is provided by the union, since they are making a profit from getting the insurance from the union. If they do not value the insurance enough to cover the costs of joining, then they will not join, since the fact will remain that they can enjoy the fruits of the union's collective wage bargaining activities without contributing to these. Even if some members did join the union as a result of the selective benefits on offer, yielding a surplus for the union that could be deployed in the production of collective benefits, why would union officials voluntarily deploy their surplus in this way? If they do, they will in effect be secular saints, giving away the surplus they have made from the supply of selective benefits to members.

Thinking carefully about it, therefore, and despite their superficial attractiveness, private benefits on offer to members should make no difference to the decision of individuals to join organizations producing collective consumption goods, provided that each individual member makes no real difference to the production of the good at issue. If the private inducements do not create a surplus for each individual, then the deficit that each incurs in dealing with the union is in effect a voluntary contribution to the cost of providing the collective consumption goods. Since people cannot be forced to contribute, they will not do so and we are back in the collective action problem. Even if some people do contribute despite this, there is no reason for those who supplied the incentives, unless they are secular saints, to go on and supply the collective goods at issue. Unless we assume that there are indeed some secular saints who actually do want to provide collective consumption goods, out of the goodness of their hearts, contributing the profits of their private activities for the benefit of others (and our core assumptions which do not envisage even partial saints do not allow us to solve the collective action problem at a stroke in this way), then selling private goods on the side provides no solution to the collective action problem.

However, circumstances do exist in which private transactions can be arranged so as to produce collective consumption goods as external effects. One example is provided by a consumer research bureau that sells findings on a range of products to subscribers on a private basis. Its research activities may contribute to a general increase in the quality of the products under investigation. This will be a good from which none can be excluded – all who buy consumer goods, whether or not they contribute to the consumer research, will benefit. The detailed findings are privately sold to subscribers, provided that the additional value of this detailed information exceeds the cost. If sufficient consumers value the additional information, then the research will be conducted and the private transactions will take place. The benefit of higher product quality will be produced as an external effect of these individually rational private transactions and will be collectively available to all. In this example, *private transactions actually produce the collective consumption good as an externality*; in Olson's example, private transactions *raise money for the collective consumption good*. The former requires no modification of our assumptions to allow for the possibility of secular saints; the latter does.

Some collective consumption goods may therefore be produced, even by utility-maximizing individuals in a state of nature, despite the fact that free riders cannot be prevented from enjoying them. There are goods that can feasibly be privatized, at a given level of technology. In addition, there are goods that can be produced as the external effects of other private transactions. It is clear, however, that there will be a considerable number of objects of desire that cannot be produced or consumed privately, and cannot be produced as external effects of private transactions. Indeed, nearly all common examples of collective consumption goods (such as collective security and clean air) fall into this category.

We do not yet, therefore, have a solution to the 'real' collective action problem, which arises from the desire of rational individuals to consume non-excludable goods involving some, but not pure, joint production. We consider two main alternatives, monarchy and anarchy, in the remainder of this chapter before going on in the next chapter to look at the role of political entrepreneurs.

### Monarchy (*Leviathan*)

In recent times, a particular construction of the work of the classical political thinker Thomas Hobbes has been associated by some political scientists with one potential solution to the collective action problem:

> The final cause, end, or design of men, who naturally love liberty, and dominion over others, in the introduction of that restraint upon themselves, in which we see them live in commonwealths, is the foresight of their own preservation, and of a more contented life thereby, that is to say, of getting themselves out from that miserable condition of war, which is necessarily consequent . . . to the mutual passions of men, when there is no visible power to keep them in awe, and tie them by fear of punishment to the performance of their covenants. (Hobbes, 1976: 173)

Hobbes's discussion of ways in which the collective action problem might be solved is well known and need not be extensively rehearsed here. Most of the essential points are presented in Chapters XVII and XVIII of *Leviathan* (1651). To get round the problem caused by free riders, men must make covenants with one another, but 'covenants without the sword, are but words, and of no strength to secure a man at all' (ibid.).

> and therefore it is no wonder if there be somewhat else required, besides covenant, to make their agreement constant and lasting; which is a common power, to keep them in awe, and to direct their actions to the common benefit.
>   The only way to erect such a common power . . . is to confer all their power and strength upon one man, or upon one assembly of men, that may reduce all their wills . . . unto one will . . . and therein to submit their wills, every one to his will, and their judgements, to his judgement. This is more than consent, or concord, it is a real unity of them all . . . made by covenant of every man with every man . . . as if every man should say to every man, *I authorise and give up my right of governing myself, to this man, or to this assembly of men, on this condition, that thou give up thy right to him, and authorise all his actions in like manner.* . . . For by this authority, given him by every particular man in the commonwealth, he

hath the use of so much power and strength conferred on him, that by terror thereof, he is enabled to perform the wills of them all, to peace at home, and mutual aid against their enemies abroad. (Hobbes, 1976: 176–7)

Men move from a state of nature to a set of political arrangements that enable them to resolve collective action problems with one agreement, and one agreement only. They give the power to enforce all agreements, including the agreement in question, to one person. This is a monarch (or Leviathan, the great whale) who is a third party to the agreement and therefore has absolutely no obligation arising from it. Since the power to enforce agreements is unqualified by any countervailing obligation, and since the monarch is not a party to the agreement that grants this power, the monarch is in effect a dictator. This is logically necessary for Hobbes's solution since, if there is a power to enforce some obligation on the monarch, *then the monarch is not a monarch.* An absolute monarch, therefore, cannot be removed from office, even if this becomes the wish of everyone else.

Thus one modern interpretation of *Leviathan* is as an account of at least one way in which the collective action problem might be solved. The monarch's power enables people to make the covenants that are a necessary precondition for any such solution. Such agreements can oblige those who favour some particular form of collective action not to free-ride once the collective action is under way, under pain of sanctions that exceed the benefit of free-riding. Such binding agreements are possible because they are enforced by a third party. If, for example, each member of a group desires some non-excludable good, such as a lighthouse, that can be efficiently produced and consumed only in concert, then they can agree amongst themselves to produce this in the confident expectation that each will fulfil his or her part of the bargain by contributing to its production. This is because they can fashion an agreement under which those who do not honour their side of the bargain will be punished. Participating in collective action becomes rational because, once agreed, it costs more than to back out of this than it is worth. Indeed the punishments meted out to those who renege on the agreement can systematically be raised until they are high enough that reneging is no longer rational. Everyone is thus made better off by the system of binding agreements since they now find themselves in a situation in which agreements are honoured and collective action problems can be resolved.

The problem that this interpretation cannot successfully address, however, is why rational people would give the power necessary to enforce all agreements to a single individual who is under no obligation to them whatsoever. A rational monarch will presumably use such power not just to enforce agreements, and maybe not even to enforce agreements at all, but to exploit subjects without mercy for personal profit. Nobody has put this argument better than John Locke did in 1690:

As if when men quitting the State of Nature entered into Society, they agreed that all of them but one, should be under the restraint of Laws, but that he should retain all the Liberty of the State of Nature, increased with Power, and made licentious with Impunity. This is to think that Men are so foolish that they take care to avoid what Mischief may be done them by *Pole-Cats*, or *Foxes*, but are content, nay think it Safety, to be devoured by *Lions*. (Locke, 1965: 372; emphasis in original)

Of course a rational monarch may enforce at least some agreements and may not be too brutally exploitative, but this will be for purely self-interested reasons, and out of no obligation to the group of subjects. Note that an absolute monarch will fear neither a revolution nor a pretender to the throne since, if such fear existed then the monarch's power would not be absolute. However, even a ruthless absolute monarch will not over-exploit subjects so badly that their falling productivity reduces their potential for efficient exploitation. For this reason alone, some collective action problems may be resolved whereas none were resolved in a state of nature. Because the state of nature is such a dismal place, people might be better off even under a moderately exploitative absolute monarchy. Faced only with the choice between a Hobbesian sovereign and a war of all against all, it might still be rational for each individual to choose the sovereign. The point, however, is that inhabitants of the state of nature might be able to do much better than this if they can possibly avoid subjecting themselves to a dictator and instead resolve collective action problems by devising some form of what Locke would call 'political society'.

It is with political society that the rest of this book is concerned. First, we consider the possibility that people might be able to organize a political society without needing to rely upon any sort of political ruler whatsoever.

**Anarchy as a solution to chaos**

Perhaps the most obvious alternative to granting a monopoly of power to one individual is to grant it to none: the 'anarchist' solution to the collective action problem. One way of doing this is to establish a system of agreements that for one reason or another enforce themselves or, in the language of rational choice theory, are 'incentive compatible'. Mutually beneficial agreements between rational individuals, including agreements to resolve collective action problems, stand little chance of success if any party to them suspects that others will not fulfil their side of the bargain. Those who produce incentive-compatible agreement may facilitate collective action by finding some way, within the agreement itself, of removing the incentive to free-ride. Such 'anarchistic' agreements are not enforced by any outside *Leviathan*, but are constructed in such a way that they still contain incentives for all parties to honour their commitments, including commitments that will be consummated at some time in the future.

There are two major reasons to be interested in anarchistic solutions to the collective action problem. The first is important for people who are ideologically interested in the notion of anarchy and in the possibility of developing a political system that does not rely upon a strong state. For those who are interested in anarchy as such, it is obviously important to find a solution to collective action problems that does not rely upon a Hobbesian *Leviathan*. The second reason is important for people who welcome or at least accept the need for a state to resolve many collective action problems, and it arises because even the most powerful state cannot address every possible collective action problem that might occur. Thus if you share a house with a number of other people, the problem immediately arises of how to keep communal areas clean, or at the very least minimally hygienic. You all might agree among yourselves about how to do this, but you are hardly going to call the police every time somebody fails to do the washing up when it is their turn. Thus, even in societies dominated by a Leviathan, much day-to-day social interaction is beyond the purview of the state and must perforce be governed along anarchistic lines.

Anarchistic solutions to collective action problems have fascinated political scientists in recent times, following in the tradition of pioneering work by Michael Taylor, set out in his book *Anarchy and Co-operation* (1976). Important texts in this tradition are Robert Axelrod's *The Evolution of Co-operation* (1984); Taylor's own revision of his work in *The Possibility of Co-operation* (1987); and Elinor Ostrom's *Governing the Commons* (1992). Two very pervasive metaphors have been used to structure discussions of the collective action problem within this tradition. The first is the Prisoner's Dilemma game and the second is the parable of the Tragedy of the Commons. I will briefly outline both of these, before returning to the main argument. (Readers familiar with them should feel free to skip ahead.)

*The Prisoner's Dilemma*

The Prisoner's Dilemma game is a traditional preoccupation of rational choice theorists, a subject upon which truly vast amounts of both thought and ink have by now been expended. The original story concerns two people, call them Jack and Jill, caught red-handed while committing some minor offence such as stealing a car. They are arrested and taken prisoner. The police know, but cannot prove, that the couple were involved in a much more serious crime, say an armed bank robbery. Jack and Jill both know that the police cannot prove their involvement in the armed robbery without a confession from one or the other of them. The two prisoners are separated and each is offered the same deal by the police. Jack's deal looks like this: 'If you give evidence against Jill and she's convicted of the armed robbery we all know you both did, then you'll walk out of here a free man. If you don't, then you'll both go to jail for stealing the car anyway. If you don't confess, and Jill does, then you'll take the whole blame for the bank job and do a long time in jail.' At the same time Jill is being offered the same incentives to confess and leave Jack taking the blame. Both Jack and Jill have been here before, however, and know the score. In particular they know that the little thing the police omitted to mention is that, if they both confess, then both with be convicted of the bank job, though they'll each get something off their jail sentence for co-operating with the forces of law and order.

The police have put Jack and Jill in a dilemma. Do they confess, hoping to walk free but risking a long jail term? Or do they stay silent, with the result that they are sure at the very least to go to jail for the car theft, and risk an even longer jail sentence if their partner does the dirty on them? Actually, they can resolve this dilemma by thinking through its logic in a systematic way, beginning by identifying the various possible outcomes and what happens to them in each eventuality. There are actually four possible outcomes – the four possible combinations of the two courses of action open to each prisoner, 'confess' or 'stay silent'. If Jack confesses, then Jill may either confess or stay silent, yielding two possible outcomes. If Jack stays silent, then Jill may either confess or stay silent, yielding two more outcomes. Each of these outcomes has implications for each prisoner, which for the sake of simplicity we can denominate in terms of years in jail. If both stay silent then both get, say, a year in jail for the stolen car. If one stays silent and the other confesses, then the one who confesses walks free – zero years in jail – and the one who stays silent and takes the blame gets ten years in jail. If they both confess, both get eight years in jail – the ten-year sentence for bank robbery less two years for co-operating with the police. These payoffs, denominated in years in jail and therefore negative, are summarized in the 'payoff matrix' shown in Figure 3.1.

This payoff matrix helps us to see that, if Jack and Jill find themselves in this situation once and once only, then both must confess. This is because, whatever the other does, each does best by confession. If Jill stays silent, then Jack does best by confessing, getting zero years in jail rather than one. If Jill confesses, then Jack does best by confessing, getting eight years in jail rather than ten. Jill faces exactly the same structure of payoffs. Thus Jack does better by confessing, regardless of what Jill does. In the language of rational choice theory, confessing is a 'dominant strategy' for Jack, where a dominant strategy is a strategy that is best, regardless of which strategy the

| | | JILL | |
|---|---|---|---|
| | | Stay silent | Confess |
| JACK | Stay silent | –1<br>–1 | 0<br>–10 |
| | Confess | –10<br>0 | –8<br>–8 |

Figure 3.1 *Two prisoners find themselves in a dilemma (Jack's years in jail bottom left, Jill's top right)*

other players choose. There is thus never a reason *not* to play a dominant strategy. Since everything is symmetrical, Jill also has a dominant strategy of confessing, doing better by confessing, regardless of what Jack does. Thus both confess. The consequence is that both do eight years in jail for the bank robbery, despite the fact that both would have been much better off staying silent and doing just a year in jail for the car theft.

The pursuit of individual self-interest has thus led to an outcome that is deplored by both. If somehow Jack and Jill could engage in collective action and both stay silent, then they would both be better off with a year in jail each. Yet each has an incentive to defect from this collective action and confess, an incentive that becomes even more attractive if it seems likely that the other prisoner will co-operate in the collective action and stay silent. In effect, the prisoner who confesses while the other stays silent is taking a free ride on the co-operation of the other, and walks out of the police station free as a bird. Fearing being double-crossed in this way, neither prisoner has any confidence that the collective action will come to pass and each confesses at the very least out of self-protection against the perfidy of the other. The net result of all this is that they are both worse off and each spends seven more years in jail than they could have got away with if collective action between them could somehow have been arranged.

Obviously, the payoffs in the game we have just been discussing are artefacts of the precise story that was told. In general a Prisoner's Dilemma is any game in which the payoffs for each player are ranked in the same way as those in the above payoff matrix. General discussions of the Prisoner's Dilemma usually describe the two strategies available to each player as 'defection' (or even just 'D') rather than confessing and 'co-operation' (or even just 'C') rather than staying silent. It is always the case in a one-off Prisoner's Dilemma game – a game that is played once, and once only – that individually rational self-interest produces an outcome, mutual defection, that is regarded by both as inferior to an alternative outcome, mutual co-operation, which could be achieved if each behaved differently. Both choose to defect, however, because defection is the dominant strategy for each. Each is better off defecting if the other co-operates, and better off defecting if the other defects. The net result is an outcome, mutual defection, that leaves both worse off.

The logic of this situation is not at all modified, as people sometimes think when they come first to this problem, by allowing the players to talk to each other, provided that agreements between them cannot be enforced by some outside agent. If they discuss matters, identify the problem, and then agree to mutual co-operation, each nevertheless has both the willingness and the ability to defect from this agreement. Each will expect the other to do likewise, and is therefore left with no alternative but to defect, leaving both worse off.

The Prisoner's Dilemma is thus a generic description of a pervasive type of collective action problem. Quite a few attempts to resolve collective action problems have thus been transformed into attempts to 'solve' the

Prisoner's Dilemma. The 'solution' that we have already canvassed, a Hobbesian *Leviathan*, works perfectly. If somebody 'outside' the game punishes players every time they defect by imposing costs greater than the benefits of defection, then the players will co-operate. They will be made better off as a result. It is not even necessary for the third party actually to impose co-operation on the players in this way, however. It is merely necessary to punish players who fail to keep their promises, whatever these promises might be, since this makes possible a binding agreement between players. The players can now see their dilemma and may promise each other that they will co-operate in collective action, in the knowledge that failure to honour their promises is not rational, given third-party punishment of this. Co-operation therefore becomes much more likely.

The 'outside' authority fulfils a role closely analogous to that of the Hobbesian sovereign. In the case of the original Prisoner's Dilemma story, this role could be filled by an organized crime syndicate. The syndicate, by arranging concrete overcoats for those who break deals made with its members, would make such deals much more likely to stick and therefore much more likely to materialize. Almost paradoxically, by threatening to kill the prisoners if they do not honour their deals with each other, the syndicate makes the prisoners much better off than they would be if there was no outside enforcer and nobody had threatened to kill them. If the players find themselves in this situation they may derive some benefits from it, but our discussion of *Leviathan* has also shown that they would never voluntarily submit themselves to absolute dictatorship by a third-party enforcer. In the case of the criminals in the Prisoner's Dilemma, the enforcer's power could easily be used to extort money from them, unless the enforcer is assumed to be entirely benevolent, a kind of saintly mobster, which seems hardly likely.

Outside enforcement is not the only way out of the Prisoner's Dilemma. Other 'solutions', however, rely upon something that we have hitherto ignored: the fact that, in many real world social interactions, the same people have the some type of interaction with each other over and over again during their respective lifetimes. If some interaction is repeated over and over again by the same players then this interaction can be described as a 'repeat-play' game, sometimes known as a 'super-game'. Taylor's crucial intuition was that *repeat-play*, as opposed to one-off, Prisoner's Dilemma games can in certain circumstances result in mutual co-operation without recourse to an outside agency. If this is the case, then the collective action problems that these games represent can be similarly 'solved', a discussion to which we will return very shortly after discussing a version of the Prisoner's Dilemma played by large numbers of people, the Tragedy of the Commons.

## The Tragedy of the Commons

The Tragedy of the Commons is a traditional parable that has been adopted by rational choice theorists as a metaphor for many manifestations of the collective action problem. Although the Tragedy of the Commons involves many people its essential structure is very similar to that of the two-person Prisoner's Dilemma. The story runs as follows. A group of farmers each has access to a piece of common pasture. Each is able to put sheep on this pasture, feeding them on its grass but retaining ownership of the sheep and therefore able to make a private profit from them. In effect, each sheep is a machine for taking shared grass from the commons and transforming this into its owner's private property. Given the physical environment of the common, grass is able to grow at a particular rate on it. If it is eaten by sheep more slowly than this rate, grass will continue to grow. If it is eaten faster than its rate of growth, then the grass will slowly disappear. If the grass is completely denuded, furthermore, it is likely that the topsoil will be washed or blown away and the common will become infertile, incapable of growing any grass or feeding any sheep. The 'tragedy' is that a group of rational farmers with access to the common may well over-graze and eventually destroy it, thereby making themselves all worse off than if they collectively limited their herds to a level that the common was capable of sustaining.

At any point in the process, each farmer faces a choice between a number of courses of action, though we here consider only two – adding another sheep to the herd on the common, or doing nothing. The outcomes of these actions depend upon the ecological state of the common. While the grass is growing faster than the sheep on the common can eat it, adding an extra sheep has no collectively damaging consequences for the farmers as a whole. The common is a collective consumption good that is jointly supplied to all farmers (since each sheep gets the same good out of it) and is not yet susceptible to crowding.

As more and more sheep are added, however, a point comes at which the sheep are eating the grass faster than it is growing. Now the addition of an extra sheep means that the grass is denuded faster than before. All of the sheep probably go a little more hungry and become a little less fat and profitable than before. In this situation, a farmer adding an extra sheep can make a net profit from doing this, getting all of the benefit of the extra sheep, but paying only a share of the costs of this in terms of the reduced productivity of the common. In the process, however, the farmer imposes a net cost on all of the other farmers, who get none of the benefit of the extra sheep but pay a share of the costs. This means that each farmer has a private incentive to graze more and more of the land, even as its productivity steadily falls as a result of ever more serious over-grazing. The result of this is that the farmers will all become worse off as the commons deteriorate, becoming severely over-grazed and possibly even suffering ecological collapse.

As the story is told, once the common is being grazed at peak capacity and if there are *n* farmers, the Tragedy of the Commons is actually an *n*-person Prisoner's Dilemma game. The co-operative course of action for each farmer at this stage in the game is not to put an extra sheep on the common; putting that sheep on the common involves defecting from this co-operation. It is a sad fact of political life that defecting and putting an extra sheep on the common is a dominant strategy for each of the farmers. If none of the other farmers puts a sheep on the common, then the defecting farmer does better by putting an extra sheep on, getting all of the benefit and paying only some of the cost. If all of the other farmers put another sheep on the common, then the defecting farmer is still better off putting an extra sheep on as well, once more getting all of the benefit of doing this but paying only some of the cost, assuming that this is not known to be the one extra sheep that pushes the entire common over the brink into ecological disaster.

As with the two-person Prisoner's Dilemma, a Hobbesian outside enforcer can help the farmers solve their collective action problem, either forcing the farmers each to put no more than a certain optimal number of sheep on the common or, more permissively, simply enforcing agreements between them and thereby allowing the farmers to do their own deals allocating quotas of sheep that will be grazed. And, as with the two-person Prisoner's Dilemma, rational farmers will be wary of giving an outside enforcer this power, fearing that this will be used for the enforcer's benefit, not their own. Finally, as with the two-person Prisoner's Dilemma, 'solutions' to the tragedy that do not depend upon an outside enforcer do depend upon there being some level of continuing interaction between the farmers, the matter to which we now turn.

## Long-term interaction, anarchy and conditional co-operation

When the same people interact over a period of time, the possibility of co-operation is much greater than if they simply have a one-shot interaction. The essential reason for this is that a vast new family of strategies emerge that are 'conditional'. In other words, I make what I do today depend upon what you did yesterday. For example and crucially in the present context, I can decide that I will co-operate with you today, *provided that you co-operated with me yesterday*, but will not co-operate with you otherwise. Taylor's (1976) pioneering analysis, subsequently followed by those of authors such as Axelrod (1984) and Ostrom (1992), showed that, if people use combinations of conditional strategies such as this, then they can in certain circumstances 'solve' the collective action problem.

### *Conditional co-operation in two-person Prisoner's Dilemmas*

For the moment, imagine one particular conditional strategy for playing a series of Prisoner's Dilemma games, where each of the individual games in the series is known as a 'stage game'. The strategy concerned is 'Tit-for-Tat', a version of the biblical 'Eye-for-an-Eye' strategy, in which I do to you today exactly what you did to me yesterday. We still need to decide what I do in the first game, before I have had a chance to observe what you did in any previous game, but imagine that I decide to co-operate in the first game. My Tit-for-Tat strategy can now be unambiguously stated: 'Co-operate in the first game; thereafter do in each game what the other player did in the previous game.' If the other player in a two-person Prisoner's Dilemma game adopts the same Tit-for-Tat strategy, then we will in this event 'solve' the collective action problem modelled by the game. I will start off by co-operating; so will the other player. Thereafter we both copy each other's move in the previous game, which in each case was to co-operate. We thus both always co-operate.

It is worth drawing attention at this point to the many, many other strategies that would have the same effect. Assume I play Tit-for-Tat. You could, for example, decide to co-operate for the first two games, then do what I did in the previous game (or two games ago). You could co-operate for the first three games, then do what I did in the previous game (or two or three games ago). You could co-operate in the first game, then co-operate as long as I co-operate but defect for the rest of eternity if I ever defect (or defect for two games, or three, or four, or five . . .). A little bit of thought will show that every single one of these strategies would, if played against my Tit-for-Tat strategy, result in continuing co-operation between us. And what is more, you would never, given sufficient ingenuity, run out of other different conditional strategies that had the same effect. In fact it turns out that there is an effectively infinite number of conditional strategies that may form part of a solution to the collective action problem, something that creates its own problems, to which we will be returning.

For the time being, however, return to two people using Tit-for-Tat strategies with each other in a repeat-play Prisoner's Dilemma game, and the stable conditional co-operation that ensues. Have we at a stroke solved the collective action problem and thereby described something akin to a perpetual motion machine or the secret of eternal youth?

Before going any further we should note that conditional co-operation of this sort will only work if the number of games played is either infinite (unlikely until the secret of eternal youth really is discovered) or indeterminate. If the number of games to be played is finite and well known, then things will start unravelling from the end. The players will know that the last game is going to offer no incentives to co-operate, since there is no possibility of subsequently 'punishing' defectors. Therefore the penultimate game will be played in the knowledge that the players will defect in the final game, and will in turn offer no initiative for co-operation. Once the end of the sequence of games is known, strategic incentives to co-operate will unravel right back to the beginning of the game. If there is no end to the sequence, however, or if the ending is arbitrary and unknown to the players (a more plausible real-life scenario) then conditional co-operation may conceivably be rational for the players.

We must next assure ourselves, however, that conditional co-operation is incentive compatible for both players on the assumptions we have made so far. To see this, imagine that we are both co-operating playing Tit-for-Tat, that we both know we are each playing Tit-for-Tat, but that you are thinking about defecting. Your defection in this game will benefit you, but will trigger a defection from me in the next game, which will cost you quite a lot. Given the payoffs in the individual Prisoner's Dilemma stage game described in the payoff matrix above, for example defecting from co-operation allows you to enjoy zero rather than one year in jail when you first defect, but then you face eight years in jail as a result of my retaliatory defection in the next round. Over the two rounds of the game, you spend eight years in jail by defecting, rather than two by co-operating. If you expect me to carry though my own Tit-for-Tat strategy, then departing from yours is not rational.

But therein lies the rub: why would you expect me to carry through my Tit-for-Tat strategy in the face of your defection? Things start to get a little complicated at this stage, but we can hold on to a few general principles. First, I no longer know precisely what strategy you are playing, except that I do know that you are not playing pure Tit-for-Tat, since you just defected after I had co-operated, when if you were playing pure Tit-for-Tat you would have co-operated. I am therefore somewhat at sea about what you are likely to do for your next move, and will probably have to observe a series of moves before I can deduce what your strategy is.

Even if I believe, for some reason, that you really are playing Tit-for-Tat and just succumbed to a little short-term temptation to defect, after which you will return to the straight-and-narrow of conditional co-operation, I still have an incentive to punish you this time, in order to remove any further temptation from you in the future. If you co-operate in the round in which I punish you by defecting, you will still see me playing Tit-for-Tat and will have no reason to suppose that I have departed from this strategy. If you retaliate to my punishment with another defection, then we will not get back on to the path of conditional co-operation, which can only be achieved by you taking your medicine and co-operating a second time, even after I punish you for your original defection. Thus it seems likely that, if you defect, I will punish you with a defection in the next round, and that you will co-operate in the third round despite this, to get us both back on the path of conditional co-operation. The net result of all this will be that your original defection will have cost you more in the long run than the short-term benefits it realized.

To get a sense of this with a practical example, imagine that you and I are sitting on a park bench, each listening to our own portable stereo system. We start off by playing the music very quietly. Each can hear their own music quite well, but each is also a little annoyed by hearing music from the other stereo. One solution for me would be to turn up my own stereo, drowning out the sound of yours. This will make me happy and you miserable, since you will barely hear your own stereo at your end of the bench unless, that is, you turn your own volume control up to match mine. Now we can each hear our stereos, but are each worse off, with more interference from the other, than we were after we were playing our stereos quietly when we first sat down on the bench. We are playing a repeat-play Prisoner's Dilemma game with each other. We each most of all would like to drown out the other, and least of all would like to be drowned out; if we each play our stereos at the same volume, we would prefer both stereos to be at a lower volume than a higher one that produces a net result verging on the unpleasant.

Imagine now that we each play a Tit-for-Tat strategy on that park bench, starting with the volume turned down low, but being resolved to turn it up should the other do so first, turning it down again should the other take the lead. In this event we will probably manage to co-operate. Obviously, if we both really do play Tit-for-Tat, the sound will stay turned down for the duration. Furthermore, you have no real incentive to defect from this. If you turn up your volume, you do get a second or two of added enjoyment but then I will surely respond by turning up my volume too. There is really no reason for me not to, since the worst thing in the world for me is to sit there being drowned out by you. Not only does turning up my volume redress the balance a little, but it sends a strong signal to you to turn your own volume down in the expectation that, if I am playing Tit-for-Tat, I will respond in kind and we will both be better off as a result. So if you turn the sound up, I respond. If you then turn the sound down, I will respond too since, if I don't, you can respond by turning your own sound up again and will have every incentive to do so. Our two Tit-for-Tat strategies do seem to be incentive compatible and to result in successful collective action between us. It is not surprising, therefore, when Robert Axelrod staged a computer tournament between various strategies for playing repeat-play Prisoner's Dilemma games, reported in *The Evolution of Co-operation*, that 'Tit-for-Tat' came out on top.

There are, however, some very important caveats we should enter at this stage. These have to do with some implicit assumptions we have made, in particular assumptions that:

- all players have perfect information about the payoffs to other players;
- players do not discount future utility 'too' heavily;
- all players know the moves made by others at every stage of the game;
- no mistakes are made by the players.

*Imperfect information about the payoffs of others*

Obviously, all payoffs to anyone from any activity are ultimately private, in the sense that only the person concerned knows how he or she feels about some particular outcome. Nobody, therefore, can have perfect information about the payoffs of others. Even apparently objective yardsticks such as a 100-dollar bill or an ounce of gold are instrumentally valued very differently by a millionaire and a pauper. And even two different millionaires are likely to have different views about how much the 100-dollar bill satisfies their fundamental private desires. This is the problem known to rational choice theorists as the problem of 'interpersonal comparison of utility' and it is not hard to see, in an intuitive way, that such comparisons are strictly speaking impossible. The problem of making such comparisons is easiest to see if we think about payoffs denominated in something that you love and I hate, for example tickets to the opera. If we are involved in some interaction in which the payoffs come in the form of opera tickets, we would be making a very serious error to analyse this as if I felt that four tickets to the opera was twice as good as two. *Au contraire*, you would do much better to work on the assumption that I was behaving as if two tickets to the opera are better than four, and that zero tickets to the opera are better still. In the same way, each of us, at a particular time and place, is likely to feel very differently about winning (or losing) an extra thousand dollars, and for anyone to operate as if we both felt the same about this would be to misunderstand the basis of what motivates our interaction.

The typical response of rational choice theorists to this problem is (sometimes) to acknowledge it and then, with a greater or lesser degree of embarrassment, to ignore it more or less completely. The main fig leaf that is used to conceal this embarrassment is a convention under which rational choice theorists tend to denominate the payoffs arising from particular outcomes in the abstract currency of 'utility', measured in 'utiles'. The often rather vaguely stated definition of utility is that it is in some sense the fundamental primitive currency of human life. Utiles are assumed to be the primitive psychological payoffs into which all real world payoffs are converted by each individual before ultimate consumption, using exchange rates that are utterly personal. Utiles, in effect, are the things that stimulate the brain in such as way as to generate those feelings of well-being and malaise that motivate people's behaviour.

Put like this it can all seem very reasonable, and utiles do seem to be the correct way to denominate the payoffs arising from human interaction if we want to be able to analyse how a particular person is going to behave in a particular situation. We can of course describe a particular human inter-action, as we have done, and write down the payoffs, in utiles (or 'points', or whatever we want to call fundamental currency in which payoffs are consumed by individuals) going to the various actors from the various possible outcomes. So far so good. We can then look at these payoffs and decide that we are looking at Prisoner's Dilemma, a Tragedy of the Commons, or indeed any other class of human interaction. As soon as we make that statement, however, we are making one of two critical logical jumps. Either we are making the type of the interpersonal comparison of utility that we have just said is impossible, assuming that all actors change 'external' real world payoffs into 'internal' utiles at some known rate. Or we are assuming that we actually know what the payoffs in utiles are, when actually we are very uncertain about this. Thus if the story of Jack and Jill's Prisoner's Dilemma is that the police punish the prisoners by confiscating their opera tickets rather than putting them in jail, and if Jack loves opera while Jill hates it, then they will not actually be playing a Prisoner's Dilemma at all, as the payoff matrix in Figure 3.2 shows quite clearly.

In contrast to the previous payoff matrix, this one is denominated in utiles accruing from confiscated opera tickets. Since Jack loves opera, every opera

JILL

|  | Stay silent | Confess |
|---|---|---|
| **Stay silent** | +1 / −1 | 0 / −10 |
| **Confess** | +10 / 0 | +8 / −8 |

Figure 3.2 *A prisoner's non-dilemma with real world payoffs denominated in confiscated opera tickets, Jill being a philistine*

ticket confiscated makes him more miserable – confiscating ten opera tickets makes him ten times more miserable than confiscating none. Jill, hating opera, has a very different view of the situation. When arrested she had ten opera tickets in her wallet and was in the very pit of misery at the prospect of having to sit through ten operas. (Sadly, her friend Jack will force her at gunpoint to do this if she has the tickets.) Every ticket confiscated makes Jill more delighted and ten confiscated opera tickets take her to the outer reaches of ecstasy, making her ten times more delighted than when only one ticket is confiscated.

We can immediately see that Jack and Jill are not involved in a Prisoner's Dilemma at all. They do both have dominant strategies, however. Jack's is the same as before, to confess, since he views a confiscated opera ticket in much the same light as a year in jail. Jill's, however, is to stay silent. Regardless of what Jack does, Jill is better off, having more opera tickets confiscated, if she stays silent. The almost certain outcome is that Jack will confess, and Jill will stay silent. This outcome, actually, gives both players their highest possible payoff, leaving Jack with all his opera tickets and Jill with none – the best that either can hope for. The police who set up that interaction would sure be barking up the wrong tree if they didn't know about how Jill felt about opera, and of course she would shed buckets of crocodile tears as they confiscated each one of her tickets.

The moral of all of this is that we can never *really* know what games we are playing with other people, since we never *really* know their payoffs and are liable to make bad mistakes if we assume that others value the same things in the same way that we do. So where does this leave our anarchistic solution to the collective action problem? If we want to be very strict about things then the problem of interpersonal comparisons of utility will be fatal to any reliance on conditional co-operation. This would probably be a little too strict for our own good, however, since we do, if we are reasonable and you are half-way normal, know that if I punch you on the nose you feel bad while if I give you a bottle of vintage champagne you feel good. In effect, I extrapolate from my own feelings to yours, on the grounds that you, in many respects, are pretty much like me. I thus feel somewhat confident when I play games with people 'like me' that I have decent information about their fundamental psychological payoffs, and therefore about what game we are playing. When I find myself dealing with someone not at all like me – a drug-crazed mugger on a dark city street, for example, or a giraffe or a Martian – then I find it almost impossible to know what game we are playing.

The bottom line is that people are much more likely to rely upon conditional co-operation, and all that flows from it, if those they are co-operating with are 'like them' in some important sense. Precisely what it means to be 'like them' depends upon the interaction involved – since it means that we feel that we have reasonable information about how the people we are dealing with will evaluate the various outcomes that are possible. In effect, while we certainly don't have to share a whole value system with the people we feel confident about co-operating with, we do have to know a fair bit about what their value system actually is, so that we have some sense of what their private desires actually are. Conditional co-operation, and the anarchistic solutions to the collective action problem that this underpins, are much more likely when a group of people have this sort of information about each other than when they are total strangers.

### The discounting of future utility

Closely related to the issue of how people turn real world outcomes into the utiles that provide their intrinsic motivations is the issue of how people feel about the future. It is almost universally assumed that people value future utility less than they value present utility, so that an effective discount is applied to future utility streams. This is probably not a bad assumption in an empirical sense, since individual behaviour does seem to conform much more closely to it than to the reverse assumption, that people value future utility more than present utility.

There is no reason why different people should not discount future utility to a different degree. This will mean that the same repeat-play game can look very different to two different people, one who discounts future utility very heavily, and another who does not. This in turn will have a considerable bearing upon the possibilities for conditional co-operation that is intended to solve collective action problems. Conditionally co-operative strategies operate to deter defection *now*, on the basis of threats of punishment *in the future*. For these threats to work, the benefits of present defection must be small relative to the costs of future punishment. Those who discount future utility very heavily may be tempted to defect if the immediate benefits they can derive from defection exceed the future (heavily discounted) costs of punishment. For a given structure of payoffs, therefore, the less an individual discounts future utility, the more likely that he or she is to find it rational to stick to a conditionally co-operative strategy, and the greater the consequent prospect of resolving the collective action problem concerned. Conversely, somebody who discounts future utility very steeply indeed may in effect view most interactions as if they are one-shot games, rendering the threats and promises inherent in conditionally co-operative strategies quite ineffective and the associated collective action problems much more difficult to resolve. Chilling fictional examples of characters with huge discount rates on future utility include assassins with terminal diseases – difficult people to deal with if they expect to be dead before they can reap the rewards of any offer being made to them.

### Imperfect information about previous moves made by other players

The issues arising from knowing how other people have actually behaved in the past are much less metaphysical than those that arise from knowing what other people's payoffs might 'really' be, or knowing how they feel about the future. It is of course self-evident that a conditional strategy, which by definition conditions one person's action on a previous action by some other person, can only work if it is clear what that previous action actually was. If people can defect from co-operation without being detected, then conditional strategies will provide no incentive whatsoever for them to co-operate.

This highlights an important difference between two-person and *n*-person interactions, one that is of great significance for the resolution of collective action problems. In a two-person interaction, if one person defects, then the other will know from her own payoffs not only that someone has defected but also precisely who that defector is. In the original two-person Prisoner's Dilemma, for example, if Jack stays silent yet finds himself being prosecuted for bank robbery, then he knows full well that Jill has confessed. He just has to look at his ten years in jail and the payoff matrix to see this. However imagine a three-person Prisoner's Dilemma involving Jack, Jill and Joe-Bob, and assume that each hates the idea of going to jail.

If nobody confesses, then they all serve one year for the car theft. If only one person confesses and two stay silent, then the two staying silent get ten years for bank robbery and the person confessing walks free. If two confess and one stays silent, then the two confessing are convicted of bank robbery, with two years off for helping the police; the person staying silent gets the full ten years. If all three confess, then all are convicted of bank robbery, getting two years off for helping the police. To give themselves an edge, the police set things up so that each of the three prisoners will be held in a different jail, so that it is not possible to know which of the others is in jail, for how long. The three-way payoff matrix is shown in Figure 3.3.

This payoff matrix shows quite clearly that, if Jack stays silent but finds himself nonetheless being prosecuted for bank robbery, then he knows with sickening certainty that *somebody* has confessed, but does not know whether it was Jill, Joe-Bob, or both. Looking at his ten years in the slammer and the payoff matrix won't help him to figure out who has made what move, since

**JOE-BOB**
**stays silent**

JILL

|  | Stay silent | Confess |
|---|---|---|
| **Stay silent** | −1 −1 −1 | 0 −10 −10 |
| **Confess** | −10 −10 0 | −8 −10 −8 |

JACK

**JOE-BOB**
**confesses**

JILL

|  | Stay silent | Confess |
|---|---|---|
| **Stay silent** | −10 0 −10 | −8 −8 −10 |
| **Confess** | −10 −8 −8 | −8 −8 −8 |

JACK

Figure 3.3　*A three-person Prisoner's Dilemma (Joe-Bob's payoffs listed in the centre of each cell)*

his ten years is consistent with three different scenarios. Unless he has eyes and ears on the street, he may never figure out what happened.

There may in practice be many collective action problems in which it is very difficult to identify free riders. Imagine a groups of farmers, for example, who all draw their water from a large common pool. Consider the fact that what goes into their farms as drinking water comes out of it, somehow or another, as sewage that must be disposed of or treated. The two main options are to let the sewage run off into the pool, or to store it and treat it. The latter is considerably more expensive. Now the pool can take a certain amount of sewage, if not exactly in its stride then at least while still providing non-lethal drinking water. If too many farmers release sewage into the common pool, however, it will become lethally polluted and supplies of drinking water will have to be brought in from afar by tanker – an extremely expensive option for all concerned. Sadly, it is possible for a farmer to release sewage into the pool in the middle of the night, and by the morning it will not be possible to identify the perpetrator of this anti-social and malodorous act.

In this situation, each farmer has an incentive to release sewage into the pool and a Tragedy of the Common Pool seems likely if nothing is done about it. The problem in this instance, however, is that conditional strategies are very much constrained by the fact that it is not possible to identify, and therefore selectively punish, defectors. Some conditional strategies are still available, for example: 'As soon as anyone pumps sewage into the pool, we all do.' The trouble with most of these, however, is that the incentives actually to carry them out are sometimes very doubtful. After all, as soon as a little bit of sewage starts floating in the water, is it really plausible to suppose that all of the others farmers will just wreck the whole lake by pumping sewage into their common pool as fast and as furiously as they can create it? We return shortly to consider the credibility of such threats. Meanwhile, we should note that the lack of information about who has made what move means that the conditional strategies available to the farmers are much blunter instruments, far less likely to succeed in resolving collective action problems.

*Mistakes*

Even the most intelligent and strategic of people do make mistakes from time to time. They may make incorrect assumptions about a world concerning which they have imperfect information. I may be playing the original Prisoner's Dilemma game with you, for example, and not realize that, unlike most normal human beings, you actually enjoy life in prison and are looking for ways to increase the amount of time you spend there. I would then come sadly unstuck. Since we always have imperfect information about important features of the decisions we must make, such mistakes are inevitable. As well as this type of mistake, however, there are blunders. These are straightforward miscalculations and logical flaws in our analysis, as well as the downright random acts we all sometimes engage in – for example one in a thousand times absent-mindedly stepping out to cross a busy road without first checking whether or not a 20-ton truck is approaching at high speed.

It might seem blindingly obvious to say that, while rational people will clearly not set out to make mistakes, nonetheless mistakes will sometimes be made. In the present context, the importance of the possibility of mistakes is that some of the conditional strategies that can help resolve collective action problems are more vulnerable to mistakes than others. It is easy to see this by looking at the Tit-for-Tat strategy that seemed to work so well at resolving the dilemma in the original Prisoner's Dilemma game. The main problem with Tit-for-Tat, indeed, is that it can go badly wrong if people make mistakes.

Imagine that we are playing a Prisoner's Dilemma game with each other and both decide to adopt a Tit-for-Tat strategy, beginning with co-operation in our first game. So far so good but, for one reason or another, perhaps just plain stupidity, some mutation in my thought processes or the effects of sunspot activity on my brain, I make a mistake in the first game and defect.

I didn't mean to but I just did. So you co-operate in the first game while I defect, unintentionally damaging you badly in the process. If we are both using a strict Tit-for-Tat strategy we are now on the road to ruin. You will copy my previous action and defect in the next game, while I will copy your previous action and co-operate. In the game after that, you will co-operate and I will defect; and so on. Working with a strict Tit-for-Tat policy, we can never get our mutual co-operation back on the rails.

Of course if I realize you are playing Tit-for-Tat like a machine and that I have made a mistake, then I can do something about it. I can get things back on the rails by co-operating twice in a row, *even after you have defected the first time*. But this, of course, is not a strict Tit-for-Tat strategy on my part, and indeed it may throw you into even more confusion about what my strategy actually is. This makes the point that strict Tit-for-Tat is extremely vulnerable to mistakes, while other strategies may be better able to cope with these. For example, the Tit-for-Tat strategy can be fitted with a safety net to protect against the worst effects of mistakes by adding a rider to the basic instructions to the effect that 'if both sides are defecting continuously, then co-operate unconditionally twice in a row every (say) ten games'. This would check every ten games whether or not some tragedy was in progress whereby two people playing Tit-for-Tat had simply got out of synchronization, being one of an enormous number of conditional strategies that would have the same broad effect. Each of these alternative strategies is in some sense more 'forgiving' than Tit-for-Tat. This raises an intriguing second-order problem, since such forgiveness can be exploited in obvious ways by a cynical opponent. There is still lots of complex strategic interaction to go into, which it is not appropriate to explore here, but the net point of it all is that it is essential for the conditional co-operation relied upon to resolve collective action problems to have some ability to withstand mistakes without plunging the players into disaster.

## Conditional co-operation in interactions between large numbers of people

The examples of Prisoner's Dilemmas that we have so far considered have been very restrictive special cases with at most three players, and where the defection of one renders the others worse off than they would have been if they had all defected. It is much more common in the real world for larger numbers of people to be involved. In such larger interactions it is very likely that the defection of any one person from mutual co-operation leaves everyone else worse off than they were before the defection, but still much better off than they would be if everyone defected. It is not at all self-evident that mutual conditional co-operation is stable in situations where, other things being equal, the remainder of the group would find it rational to continue co-operating after one or more members have defected.

The problem arises because, in contrast to the situation in the two-person Prisoner's Dilemma game, a potential defector will know that co-operation will remain rational for the rest of the players even after someone has defected. Knowing this, defection and free riding become attractive once more, even in repeat-play games. Every rational member of the group will think this and collective action will collapse. It is not hard to see that this is the 'real' collective action problem. While we cannot draw the multi-dimensional payoff matrix to show the game as we did before, the logic of this situation is relatively straightforward. Each individual thinks as follows: 'If I and only I defect, then it will remain rational for the others to co-operate in future games since they do better by doing this than by defecting. I do better by defecting in this case. If so many others defect that it is no longer rational for the remaining players to continue co-operating in future games, then it is no longer rational for me to continue co-operating. I do better by defecting in this case too. Thus the only situation in which I should co-operate is if the co-operation of the rest of the group is at some threshold of viability, so that my co-operation in this game does make a difference to the incentives for the rest of the group to co-operate in future games.' Thus an individual group member will co-operate only when such co-operation is 'pivotal' to collective action, given his or her assumptions about the strategies of the other players. 'Pivotal' in this sense means that the individual's choice of strategy makes the difference in future games between whether or not there will be the co-operation of enough of the rest of the group to generate valuable collective action.

This line of thinking shows us the logic linking the possibility of co-operation to the size of the group concerned. Other things being equal, the larger the group, the less likely any individual member is to regard his or her co-operation as pivotal. The smaller the group, the more likely this is.

Another very important implication of the same logic is that some free-riding can be tolerated by any group, provided that the residual group of providers is large enough to engage in worthwhile collective action. This does carry the implication, however, that if nothing is done about it free-riding will continue to be rational until the group of co-operators has shrunk to such a small size that further defection will render future collective action non-viable, so that the next putative free rider is in fact pivotal. This seems to suggest that collective action in such circumstances may be very sub-optimal, operating at a level that is barely viable because, at that point, defection of anyone else is no longer rational. Why in such circumstances, furthermore, would rational actors not rush to be the first free riders, leaving a group of suckers locked into this barely viable collective action from which everyone benefits?

To put some substantive flesh on these theoretical bones, imagine that ten of us are protected by a dike that, after heavy rain, has sprung three leaks. Each leak can be stopped if someone puts a hand into it, but an unattended leak will quickly spell disaster and the end of the dam. Collective action by three people is thus needed to save the dike. If I am one of the ten, why don't I just go straight to bed, leaving the remaining nine to sort out which three will spend a cold wet night with their hand in the dike? Others of my ilk may go to bed too, but when there are only three people left, they will have no choice – either they each do the job or we all drown. They will no doubt feel fed up with the free riders, thinking murderous thoughts as they sit up all night in the pouring rain, but they won't be suicidally mad enough to prefer drowning to being played for a sucker. The danger, of course, is that there may be a rush to bed as soon as the situation becomes clear, leaving fewer than three people to fix the dike, and ten dead free riders.

The key to all of this is that it may well be that, in large groups of individuals, it will be self-evident that no one individual is pivotal to the possibility of collective action. Conditionally co-operative strategies may not solve this because they are not necessarily 'incentive compatible'. While it is always possible to say that you will defect from co-operation if anyone else defects, actually to do this may be to cut off your nose to spite your face. The larger the group, the less significant any single defection and the more likely this is to happen.

**Threats, promises and co-operation**

The discussion in the previous section has suggested that, while conditionally co-operative strategies may resolve certain collective action problems, especially for very small groups, they may not solve many collective action problems for large groups in which no single individual is pivotal. In such cases potential free riders may well figure that, whatever the rest of the group says, they can defect anyway and simply challenge the rest of the group to cut off their noses to spite their faces.

This problem has arisen, in part, because one course of action open to the participants has been ignored. This is to threaten potential free riders with dire consequences if they pursue the course of action that rational self-interest would otherwise indicate. Before pursuing this argument any further, we need to be quite clear about the nature of threats and promises.

If I threaten you, or make a promise to you, then the sentence conveying the threat or promise has the grammatical structure: 'If you do X, then I will do Y.' If I make a threat, then the Y that I threaten will impose costs on you. If I make a promise, then the Y that I promise will give benefits to you. But a threat or a promise is logically much more than a conditional statement such as this. If it is to influence your behaviour, as compared to the situation in which the threat or promise had not been made, then Y must be something that I would not otherwise do if you did X. If it was not, I would do it anyway and the threat or promise would not influence your behaviour. From this we can see quite clearly that threats and promises imply courses of action which, other things being equal, the person making them would prefer not to carry out.

To get a sense of this, go back to the original Prisoner's Dilemma game but imagine that one prisoner must declare what he or she is going to do before the other. Imagine we are playing this and the police have set things up so that you have to declare what you are going to do first. Before the game starts, I could say: 'If you talk to the police first, then I will talk to the police too.' This is not really a threat, since I am merely reciting my dominant strategy – if I had said absolutely nothing, you would have assumed I would do this and have acted accordingly. If I make the threat, you would be justified in thinking: 'I know that, why is he telling me this?' There is a real promise that I could make, however; I could say: 'If you stay silent, then I'll stay silent too.' This is a real promise since, other things being equal, I would actually prefer not to carry it out when the time comes. I might induce you to stay silent by making the promise, but I then have a strong incentive to break my promise and talk to the police anyway. You will know this of course, and may well take my promise with a giant pinch of salt.

To see a real threat in action, imagine that I expect some students to write me an essay, and that the university's rules are that, if a student does not hand in an essay by the deadline, then they will get a zero mark. Imagine, furthermore, that I tell some student who owes me an essay: 'If you don't do the essay by the deadline, then I'll give you a zero mark.' When I utter these words, I am just stating the rules of the game and not changing its structure in any way. This is not really a threat. But imagine that I said: 'If you don't do your essay on time I'm going to kick you round the lecture hall till I break every bone in your body.' Now *that's* a threat! The strategic key to it is that, while I want the student to heed the threat and do the essay on time, if the student doesn't hand in the essay I will not, being a mild-mannered sort of fellow, actually want to kick the laggard round the lecture hall with such disastrous effect. Quite apart from anything else I would probably get the sack. If the students believe me, it may affect their behaviour – but why *should* they believe me since I clearly have no incentive actually to carry out the threat?

Thus, for a threat to be more than just a restatement of the existing payoffs in whatever game we are playing – for a threat to *change* game play in some material way – whatever is being threatened must be something that would not have happened anyway in the normal course of events. Since I will always do what I most want to do in the normal course of events, my threats must involve conditional statements that I will *not* do what I most want if you fail to carry out some action that I desire, in an attempt to induce you to carry out that action. In this sense threats and promises are exactly the same strategic moves. If I am a sadist who positively enjoys kicking students around lecture halls and who, other things being equal, would choose to do this every afternoon as an enjoyable way to pass the time, then my threat to kick students round the room if they don't hand in their essays on time is more of a promise *not* to kick them around the room if they *do* hand their essays in on time. Of course, if they know me to be a sadist, the credibility of my promise among students now turns upon the extent to which they believe that I will *not* kick them around the room even if they do hand in their essays on time.

All of this highlights an intriguing paradox that lies at the heart of any discussion of threats or promises. A threat to do something that the threatener wants to do anyway seems redundant; a threat to do something that the threatener does not want to do anyway seems incredible. The same can be said of promises, which have just the same logical structure as threats, save for rewarding rather than punishing the recipient. Why would rational people ever make or heed threats or promises?

The answer to this puzzle can be found by paying a return visit to the notion of 'reputation'. In this context, the important aspect of reputation is a reputation for doing what you say you will do. In other words, if you have such a reputation, then people who deal with you know that you have a history of doing what you said you would do, of carrying out threats and honouring promises for example, even when you had a short-term incentive not to do so. Why would people not just think you stupid for doing this? If we consider only one game played in isolation, then the issue of reputation does not arise. You choose some course of action, and that is the end of things. If several games are being played over a period of time, however, then what happens in previous games may be known to those playing subsequent games.

Go back to our Prisoner's Dilemma and imagine that I have a reputation for doing what I say I will do, regardless of the consequences in any particular game. My reputation is built on a past track record of always doing what I say I will do and has the interesting and important property that, while a reputation can take a long time to build, it can be lost very quickly if in some game I say I will do one thing and then do something else. *Now* I promise you that if you stay silent then I will also stay silent when it comes to my turn, despite the incentives that I will then have to talk to the police. If you believe me then you will indeed stay silent; and if I honour my promise then we will both be better off than if you don't believe me and confess. My reputation has helped us both! It is a valuable asset for me and, if you know that I will be playing many games in the future, you may well figure that I am very unlikely to destroy this valuable asset merely for the short-term benefits of double-crossing you in a single game.

To get a feel for this in terms of the original parable of the Tragedy of the Commons, imagine a group of ten farmers who are grazing sheep on common land and who each adopt a conditional strategy of the following form. 'We will each put 100 sheep on the common, making 1,000 sheep in all. As soon as more than 1,000 sheep appear on the common, we will know for sure that one of us has defected, even if we don't know who this is. We will all then feel free to put as many sheep as we like on the common for three months, after which we will restore the quota of 100 sheep each.' Think of me as a sneaky farmer – I put another five sheep on the common and, just as the others find out and are about to let things rip I argue as follows. 'Surely you're not going to cut off your noses to spite your faces; I know having 1,000 sheep on the common is best, but we're better off living with 1,005 sheep than just letting things rip and losing a fortune for three months.' Having regard to reputation, however, each other farmer might well reply thus: 'If we take a short-term view of course you're right, Mr Sneaky but if we don't carry out our threat now, then nobody will believe us in the future. If we are to resolve our collective action problems, then we must be able to make credible threats, and the only way to make future threats credible is to carry out the threats we make now, even if we'd prefer not to do so.'

I don't have the space here to go into the fascinating and important topic of how to build and maintain a reputation, and of the value this might have. What we need to appreciate in this context is that reputations do make a difference, and can help people resolve collective action problems by opening up the possibility of making *credible* threats and promises.

Beyond this, a few very general comments are in order. For obvious reasons, reputations will be easier to build and maintain among smaller rather than larger groups of people, and particularly among groups of people whose membership is relatively stable. Even in these groups, of course, if there is a huge short-term incentive for people not to do what they say they will do, then this may tempt some to ruin their reputations and suffer the consequences. But, when people expect to interact with each other over long periods of time, reputations can be very valuable commodities and it may be that there is almost no real world situation that can generate high enough incentives to tempt someone to put their reputation at risk.

In large and/or unstable groups the likelihood is much less that people will be able to build reputations themselves, or will know reliably about the reputations of others. The contribution of reputation to resolving collective action problems by allowing people to make credible threats and promises will consequently be much less in larger and/or less stable groups and, for this reason alone, collective action may be much harder to organize.

## Choosing between strategies for co-operation: the role of norms

I indicated above that there are typically very many possible conditionally co-operative strategies that people can choose when involved in a particular interaction. I illustrated these with just a tiny selection of the huge number of variations we can imagine to the basic Tit-for-Tat strategy. We also saw that there are typically many, many ways for the players to combine such strategies and find an equilibrium in the game, and that many of these equilibria can involve ongoing mutual co-operation.

This creates an intriguing paradox. The Prisoner's Dilemma game that we are taking to model many important forms of human interaction does not result in mutual co-operation if it is played once and once only, without outside enforcement. When the game is played over and again by the same players, the problem of co-operation takes a startling new form – rather than being no incentive-compatible strategies that result in mutual co-operation, there are now in a sense too many of them. For mutual co-operation to ensue, it is still necessary for the players to select strategies that combine to produce this, yet they have a huge number of possible strategies to choose from. The problem is now for people to co-ordinate on combinations of strategies that do indeed result in mutual co-operation.

As a very simple example, consider the problem of which side of the road to drive your car on. There is a strong incentive to engage in collective action here, to produce an outcome in which everyone travelling in one direction drives on one side of the road, while everyone travelling in the other direction drives on the other side of the road. Despite transient incentives to drive on whichever side of the road is the most convenient at the time, the costs of everyone doing this are immense. Two obvious driving strategies are: always drive on the left; always drive on the right. Of course these are only two strategies among many possibilities. For example you might choose to drive on the left on even days of the month and drive on the right on odd days, or to drive on the left on the night of a full moon but on the right otherwise, or whatever.

If all drivers opt to drive on the left, or if all drivers opt to drive on the right (or indeed if they all adopt either of the other two sample strategies mentioned, including the one about the full moon), then this results in mutually valuable collective action. But if some drivers opt for one strategy (driving on the left, say) and some opt for the other (say driving on the right) then they are all collectively and individually in serious trouble. They care very much about the need to co-ordinate on a single strategy but may well care very little about which strategy they actually choose to co-ordinate on. If there is a widely known convention that people drive on the right, then this co-ordination problem is resolved; no non-suicidal driver has an incentive to do other than drive on the right. We can think of such conventions as 'norms' and it is not hard to see how norms might well help people to identify combinations of strategies that result in mutually beneficial collective action.

Of course the problem of which side of the road to drive on presents a very benign view of the role of norms, since the main interest of most people is simply to co-ordinate on a driving strategy and avoid lethal head-on collisions. Norms may often be far more controversial than this if some strategies are more beneficial to some people while other strategies are more beneficial to others.

Consider the problem of leaving a sinking ship that can be evacuated without loss of life if this is done in an orderly manner. If everyone tries to leave the ship at the same time, the lifeboats cannot cope; they may jam and many may die in the ensuing chaos. If everyone does not leave at the same time, then this implies that some people leave before others; in this event the chances of everyone getting off the ship alive are vastly increased. There is a collective action problem, which may be resolved by adherence to a norm about who should leave a sinking ship first. When the *Titanic* was sinking, at least according to the movies, the norm was 'women and children first'. Of course, since the passengers on a sinking ship can never be completely certain that they will all get off safely if they follow the norm, the precise substance of this norm may well be controversial – 'able-bodied males first' seems a perfectly good norm to me. Since I have not seen a movie that was made about a ship that sank in recent times, I do not know whether or not the 'women and children first' norm has been abandoned on sinking ships in response to demands for equality of the sexes. What is quite clear, since this norm does leave some people in a better position than others, is that its observance will be a matter of dispute when the sea gets really rough.

## In conclusion

We have seen that rational people may desire fruits of collective action that they will be unlikely to gain if others always behave according to the dictates of selfish utility-maximization. This creates a collective action problem to which there are several potential solutions.

In the first place, the problem may solve itself if the goods in question are such that they require the unanimous co-operation of consumers in order to be produced at all. In the second place, some fruits of collective action may be easily 'privatized' by the adoption of cheap and simple exclusion mechanisms and provided only to those who contribute to them. In the third place, some collective action may take place anyway as an external effect of private transactions. In none of these cases do we really have a problem and we may wish to think of the 'real' collective action problem as applying to those goods to which these potential solutions do not apply.

These are things that people desire which require collective action by some but not all of the group, from which it is expensive or difficult to exclude people, and which are not produced as a spin-off from some other form of activity. These conditions will apply to many of the things that people desire, especially those that require collective action by moderate or large groups if they are to be generated.

The provision of such goods may be facilitated by a strong ruler, or *Leviathan*, but rational people would fear that someone with power over the group in this way would become a dictator. Only a secular saint would use power over the group for the benefit of the group itself rather than exploiting the group for or personal gain. Failing a saint or philosopher king, there are some forms of valuable collective action that materialize on a 'self-policing' or anarchistic basis. We have seen that these are more likely in small and stable groups, but that even in such groups there may be forms of valued collective action that are unlikely to emerge. We move on in the next chapter to look at another possible way of resolving collective action problems, which depends upon the activities of 'political entrepreneurs'.

# 4

# Political Entrepreneurs, Politicians and Parties

The 'solutions' to the pervasive problem of collective action reviewed in the previous chapter depend either upon the existence of an autocratic Hobbesian sovereign to enforce co-operation from outside the group, or upon anarchistic conditional co-operation within a small and stable community. The problem with a Hobbesian sovereign is that there seems to be no reason, absent a saint or a philosopher king, why an absolute monarch will not exploit subjects without mercy, leaving them little better off than they would be in a state of nature, in a war of all against all. The problem with anarchistic conditional co-operation is that, however conceived, it seems a far more plausible solution for small and stable groups of people, for *communities* in which an individual action is more likely both to make a difference and to be noticed, than it is in larger and less stable groups. This leaves us with the question of how most collective action problems are resolved in the real world, a social world that extends far beyond small, stable communities and in which large collections of people with a continuous turnover of membership are the rule rather than the exception.

One important possibility involves members of the group hiring an outsider to act as an 'enforcer'. This person is in effect a leader contracted as an agent of the group, with specified and limited powers that extend for a fixed period of time, rather than a permanent Hobbesian sovereign with absolute power over all. Members of the group cede sufficient coercive resources to this leader to deal with free-riding by individuals or small groups, but not sufficient to allow the leader to subjugate the group as a whole. This means that the group cannot be 'too' small, in a sense that we will return to in more precise terms. The hired leader will in effect be a political entrepreneur providing, for reward, 'political services' that help the group resolve their collective action problems.

If the incumbent political entrepreneur is to be effective at resolving collective action problems, however, getting rid of an incumbent must be beyond the scope of any one individual group member and must therefore inevitably confront the group with second-order collective action problems. Resolving these is crucial to the effectiveness of using political entrepreneurs to resolve the first-order collective action problems that they are originally hired to tackle. We will see below, however, that members of a group may have a reasonable expectation that the second-order problem of evicting renegade entrepreneurs can be resolved, as a result of competition between hopeful candidates for the incumbency.

In the second half of this chapter we look at the incentives for aspiring political entrepreneurs to collude, banding together into alliances which we might think of as 'political parties', in order to enhance their chances of landing lucrative contracts to supply political services to large groups.

## What do political entrepreneurs do?

In the plot of a thousand western movies, a small community of decent townsfolk is terrorized by a gang of villains who make everyone's life a living hell. The bad guys gamble, fight, drink, rape and pillage till decent people just can't stand it any longer. The townsfolk, being far more numerous, could of course gang up on the villains and run them out of town if only they all got together. But each individual solid citizen is scared of being personally and painfully gunned down in the confrontation. None of them is prepared to take that risk, each preferring to sit at home while others stop the bullets. Since all townsfolk think the same way, their nightmare continues.

The folk in our western town face a collective action problem. What do they do in the movies? They send for a hired gun – a really tough, fair and ruggedly handsome stranger, with whom they agree a contract to run the villains out of town. Having been sent for in some distant burg, the hired gun

- rides into town covered in trail dust;
- has a bath and several well-earned shots of rot-gut whiskey;
- takes the townsfolk's money;
- runs the villains out of town while local lily-livers look on fearfully from behind their curtains;
- rides off into the sunset, slightly wounded;
- breaks at least one local heart in the process.

The bath, the whiskey and the broken heart are not strictly relevant to the argument under construction. The 64,000-dollar question is: 'Why does the hired gun actually ride off into the sunset as promised, rather than putting on a dirty black hat and becoming the new bad person in town?' After all, the hired gun presumably has the power – and we might also imagine the incentive – to gamble, fight, drink, rape and pillage just as much as any professional villain.

In the movies, the answer to this question has to do with *reputation*. The hired gun makes a living running bad people out of town *and riding off into the sunset* – the riding off into the sunset part of the deal is just as important as the running bad people out of town. As soon as some enforcer fails to ride off into the sunset but sticks around to become the new depraved villain, word gets around. Other towns in torment show a marked reluctance to send for the enforcer in question. Work in the enforcement business gets hard to come by for the renegade lawman. Furthermore, as long as there are plenty of young guns waiting in the wings to become the next generation of enforcers, the renegade enforcer can easily be run out of the town he never left by yet another enforcer. It's a hard life for a hired gun in the Wild West so it's better, in the medium and longer term, to build up a reputation as an awesome individual who does indeed ride off into the sunset when the bad people have been run out of town. If there is no competition from hungry young guns, of course, then the prospect of sticking around to rape and pillage will look altogether more attractive.

Hired guns are examples of what we will think of in the rest of this chapter as political entrepreneurs, people who contract with a group to supply externally enforced solutions to collective action problems. Political entrepreneurs are not Hobbesian sovereigns. While it is an essential part of their job that they have enough firepower to solve collective action problems by coercing free riders as individuals or even as small groups, it is equally part of their job that they do not have enough firepower to resist any concerted assault by group members, or to fight off some new young gun that the group might hire, should the incumbent entrepreneur decide to renege on the original deal and exploit the group. Given the distinct possibility of being run out of town and being thrown back on the job market with a big black mark on their reputation, potential competition between entrepreneurs provides strong incentives for incumbent entrepreneurs to honour the promises that they have made.

(The role of a gun in the Wild West, and indeed in real life, is most interesting in this context, since a gun quintessentially allows a 'weak' person to kill a 'strong' one and in this way undermines the role of any putative Hobbesian sovereign. Alas we have neither the time nor the space here to explore the political theory of guns.)

The movie Wild West, of course, is a modern metaphor for the state of nature. In westerns the government, as far as it comes into the story at all, is always far removed from the action, of little help when problems arise. Most western storylines are about how to survive in a cruel world without useful access to government. For the most part people solve their own collective action problems by agreement, or they hire a sheriff from their midst to keep law and order. This works in the stable population of a small town, who enjoy their anarchistic idyll until bad people ride in from another social planet, people with no incentive to respond to the anarchistic conditionally co-operative strategies of townsfolk. When law and order break down as a result, a typical response is to contract with an 'outside' enforcer in the form of a hired gun.

Moving beyond the movies, the possibility of contracting for the services of a political entrepreneur does more generally offer a potential way out of many troublesome collective action problems. The entrepreneur supplies 'political services' for a fee. These services may include enforcing agreements made by group members, imposing sanctions on free riders, or getting more deeply involved in the co-ordination and generation of collective action – for example by identifying strategies that allow group members to generate collective action, or even producing goods and services directly and using limited powers of coercion to 'tax' the group with enforced payments for these. To save ink, let's call the 'political entrepreneur' a *politician* and the 'group to which political services are supplied' the *public*. The portfolio of political services that are provided might be thought of as a *regime*.[1]

Note that the concept of 'political services' deployed here is much broader than the more conventional notion of public goods that we have used up until now. The term 'public goods' tends to be used to refer to certain objects of people's desires – things people want, yet from which they cannot be excluded and to which they therefore need not contribute. The notion of political services includes the direct provision of public goods but in addition encompasses the provision of more general political regimes that facilitate the production of public as well as other goods and services that might otherwise be available only sub-optimally to the 'client' group. Whether public goods are produced directly, or whether a regime is put in place that facilitates their production by private individuals or groups, the end product is the same. The outcome is the resolution of collective action problems as a result of the provision of what I am referring to here as 'political services'.

One point is quite clear: groups of rational people will never give to some individual the power to coerce them *as a group*. This is because there is no reason to suppose that such power will not be used to exploit them mercilessly, while the group will have no recourse against a renegade entrepreneur with the power to coerce them all. All-powerful political entrepreneurs will be Hobbesian sovereigns who will have little incentive to supply any of the political services that they have contracted for, since they can raise revenue by coercion whether they produce these services or not. They will have to do enough to keep group members productive victims of exploitation, but will need to pay no more attention than this to the private desires of group members. A political entrepreneur with the power to coerce the group *en masse* is thus a dictator, and we have already seen that it is unlikely to be rational for group members to submit themselves to a dictator.

So the only balance of forces that is simultaneously attractive to both aspiring political entrepreneurs and to members of a group desiring the otherwise forbidden fruits of collective action is one that gives the entrepreneur sanctions that are powerful enough to coerce individuals or small sub-groups, but not the entire population. The political entrepreneur may then use these sanctions to counteract rational tendencies to take free rides. Giving political entrepreneurs 'enough' but not 'too much' power in this way does involve making important assumptions about the nature of political power and the size of the groups that will find it rational to deal with political entrepreneurs. The ceding by the public of coercive power to a politician is, of course, conditional upon satisfactory provision of agreed political services. Retrieving this power from renegade politicians who have failed to honour their side of a bargain will, however, still present the public with collective action problems.

## 'Contracts' between the public and politicians

The relationship between a politician supplying political services and the public to which these services are supplied thus takes the form of a 'contract'. This contract lasts for a fixed period of time and specifies the powers to be granted to the politician during this period, the political services to be provided and the other rewards due to the politician in exchange for these services. This sounds straightforward enough but, since we are talking about contracts ceding real coercive powers in return for facilitating the provision of valuable *political* services, at least four complications arise. The first concerns how the public awards the contract to the politician in the first place. The second concerns whether limits can in fact be placed on the coercive power that is ceded by the public to the politician. The third concerns the incentives which politicians have to renege on their contracts with the public once these have been awarded. The fourth concerns whether even politicians with limited powers can be evicted from office if they do indeed renege on their contract with the public.

### Who awards the contract to supply political services?

Although we talk of 'the' public, the fact of the matter is that the public is a 'they' not an 'it'.[2] This means that we must not become too glib about how 'the public' might make a contract with a politician. One way to avoid such glibness is to force ourselves always to talk about 'members of the public', rather than the public. As soon as we begin to think about how a collection of different members of the public might decide among themselves whether and how to make a contract with a politician to supply political services, we see that the matter is far from straightforward. We will consider collective decision-making in greater detail in the following chapter so here I will present no more than a sketch of the type of process that might result in the award of a contract to supply political services by members of the public.

The essential underlying feature of the process of awarding such a contract will be the coercive balance of forces between sub-groups in the public as a whole. (In future I will refer to any sub-group of the public as a whole as a 'faction'.) Despite the possibility that there may be certain basic political services – peace and the enforcement of agreements, perhaps – that almost all members of the public value, there will very likely be a divergence of tastes within the public on matters that all consider to be important. Ultimately, any faction or alliance of factions that can prevail over the remainder of the public regardless of their opposition will be able to deal with a political entrepreneur and make a contract for the provision of a political regime for the public as a whole.

A faction may find itself in this position for a number of reasons. First, it may in fact be able to coerce the remainder of the public if need be – in this case we may think of the dominant faction as possessing more coercive resources than the rest of the group put together. Second, even a faction that does not control more coercive resources than the rest of the group may be able to dominate the remainder of the public if that remainder cannot agree upon what it prefers. A particular faction may for example face two others, one that wants a more comprehensive political regime than the one in question, while the other wants a less comprehensive one. The faction that prefers a regime 'in between' those wanted by the others may be able to prevail over the two other factions. Third, some faction may face a collection of people who would be potentially far more powerful if only they were able to exploit their combined coercive resources, but who in practice simply cannot organize the collective action necessary to do this.

We can summarize in one simple principle the three main reasons why one particular 'in' faction may be able to make a contract for the supply of a political regime to the public as a whole. An 'in' faction, or alliance of factions, can contract as the dominant faction to impose a regime on the public as a whole if it does not face an 'out' faction, or alliance of factions, that between them

- can collectively impose their will on the 'in' faction if they choose to do so and;
- can agree on some alternative regime that they all prefer to the regime favoured by the 'in' faction.

The essential criterion is therefore that members of a particular in faction or alliance will prevail as the sub-group capable of contracting political services for the group as a whole unless they can be beaten; and they can be beaten if there is an out faction or alliance that has the common purpose, organization and coercive power to do this.

As an important aside it is worth noting that we have deliberately said nothing about the possibility that particular factions might be 'neutral' or 'abstain' in crucial struggles for the control of political regimes. This is because our analysis simply does not recognize the notion of neutrality in this context. The intervention of a particular faction either makes a difference to the outcome of such a struggle or it does not. When it does not make a difference this means that, if the faction intervenes the outcome is A and, if the faction does not intervene the outcome is also A. The faction is thus irrelevant, not neutral. If the intervention does make a difference, then intervening produces outcome A, while not intervening produces outcome B. In this event, *not* intervening cannot be said to be 'neutral' in any normal sense of the word. The decision not to intervene is a decision to bring about outcome B rather than outcome A, when the opposite was in the power of the decision-maker. There is no difference at the end of the day in producing outcome B as a result of passively not intervening, or as a result of actively intervening. The 'neutral' actor has made just as much substantive difference to the outcome. In this important sense there are no neutral actors in important struggles for political control. There are pivotal actors, whose actions can make a difference; and there are non-pivotal actors, whose actions cannot make a difference. A non-pivotal actor by definition is irrelevant to the outcome; a pivotal actor can never be neutral. Put rather more unkindly, only an irrelevant actor has the luxury of being strategically 'neutral'.

The next chapter discusses in more detail how groups of people might make decisions; here what we can say is that there will be a political struggle, as a result of which individuals comprising a subset of the group as a whole will emerge with the power both to make deals on behalf of the group and to impose these forcibly on the group as a whole if need be. It is this subset that negotiates the contract with the political entrepreneur for the supply of a political regime for the public at large. Other members of the public may feel dissatisfied with this but the bottom line is that they can be coerced into reluctant acceptance if need be. Ultimately, it is the physical and political ability to engage in such coercion – more typically of course the recognition of this ability by all concerned without the need to put it brutally to the test – that identifies the 'in' faction or alliance that is in a position to do deals with aspiring political entrepreneurs.

*Can the coercive power ceded to politicians be limited?*

Fundamental to the distinction between a political entrepreneur and a Hobbesian absolute monarch is that the coercive power in the hands of the political entrepreneur is limited. Specifically, this power must be sufficient to allow the entrepreneur to fulfil the contract to supply political services, which will involve the power to coerce individual free riders, but it must not be sufficient to allow the politician to coerce the group as a whole. Is it realistic to assume that the coercive power ceded to politicians can be constrained in this way?

As might be expected, my answer to this question is that it is indeed realistic to assume that coercive power can be limited, but further consideration of why this might be a reasonable answer does qualify the argument about entrepreneurs as a whole in one very important respect.

Ultimately, the discussion of how political entrepreneurs might help resolve collective action problems depends upon an *assumption* that, as a matter of physical force, a group of people can be large enough so that no individual political entrepreneur can coerce that group *en masse*. Obviously, a very strong individual can coerce a very small group *en masse* and hence be their absolute monarch. Genghis Khan can coerce just you and me utterly and completely and, for this precise reason, you and I would not rationally take action that ceded power to Genghis Khan. If he conquered us anyway, despite out best efforts to resist this, he would indeed be our absolute monarch and would exploit us on his terms, not ours. But, depending of course upon the precise coercive technology that is available, a group can be large enough that no politician can physically coerce them *en masse*. Certain technologies do make it easier for politicians to coerce larger groups *en masse* but, as I hinted above in an aside on the political role of guns, other technologies make it possible for even 'weak' group members to kill 'strong' politicians. For a given state of coercive technology, therefore, the assumption is that a group can be large enough for an incumbent politician to be unable, as a matter of physical force, to coerce the group *en masse*.

What this discussion shows us is that political entrepreneurs will only offer an attractive solution to collective action problems for groups that are large enough, in this important sense, to resist mass coercion. Members of smaller groups will fear that ceding power to a political entrepreneur will in effect cede power to an absolute monarch. Indeed they may well not cede power at all but actually be conquered physically by a powerful outsider, quite regardless of their wishes. Such groups may be small enough to be able to organize the type of anarchistic conditional co-operation that we discussed in the previous section, although there is no guarantee of this. The real problem faced by groups that are small in this sense is the strong possibility that they will be physically conquered and enslaved by external monarchs, politicians and other groups. This possibility, indeed, does not augur well for the independent survival prospects of groups that are 'small' in this sense and I will not consider them further in this discussion. We will in what follows concentrate on the role of political entrepreneurs in groups that are large enough, for a given level of coercive technology, to resist physical coercion *en masse* by a single incumbent.

Astute readers will notice that I have in fact *assumed away* the problem of the Hobbesian sovereign when I assume that a group can be large enough to resist physical coercion *en masse* and have inferred from this that only groups that are large in this sense will avail of the services of a political entrepreneur. Hobbesian sovereigns will of course remain very relevant indeed for small groups which, given the current level of technology, cannot resist exploitation *en masse*. Indeed by definition such groups will be unable to resist conquest and subsequent exploitation by free-ranging Hobbesian sovereigns.

It is also important to remember, however, that I have thus far been dealing with the raw *physical* ability to coerce a group *en masse*, as opposed to the *politics* of successfully doing this. It may well be that a group whose members are very dissatisfied with the exploitative behaviour of some incumbent politician and who are well able, as a matter of physical force, to combine to throw the rascal out, are not able, politically, to organize this among themselves. Groups may thus be exploited because of their political as opposed to physical weaknesses, a matter to which I shortly return, having first considered why politicians who are not all-powerful may nonetheless fail to honour their agreements with the public, and hence create incentives for the public to throw them out of office.

*Incentives for politicians not to honour their contracts
with the public*

Once a contract has been agreed for the supply of political services, problems are likely to arise almost immediately, not least because politicians face obvious incentives to under-perform, giving short measure on what they have agreed to supply to the public. This is because, while in theory the politician is no more than an agent of the public, with members of the public being the principals in the relationship, in practice an incumbent politician will be in a very much better position to know what is going on, in relation to the political services that have been contracted for, than any member of the public. (For an excellent general introduction to the economics of the 'principal–agent' approach, see Kreps, 1990: Ch. 16.) In order to know that they are getting what they bargained for, members of the public need to *monitor* the behaviour of the incumbent. But effective monitoring is both costly and difficult, presenting collective action problems for members of the public. Furthermore, if the monitoring reveals serious under-performance, then changing political leaders is also costly. There are the costs of identifying and negotiating a contract with a new politician, and there is the administrative disruption that attends any change of regime. All of this means that an incumbent politician will almost certainly be able to use his or her position to give short measure, to 'shirk' somewhat on the deal with the public. This will be because such shirking may not be detected and because as long as the costs of replacing the incumbent are higher than the benefits, members of the public have no real incentive to repudiate the contract, however fed up they may be with the situation.

Incumbent politicians do face limits on their ability and incentives to shirk on their deals with the public. Even without a rival politician waiting in the wings and ready to offer an alternative and more attractive package of political services, political entrepreneurs may deliver on their promises for reasons that are explored extensively by Albert Hirschman in his influential book, *Exit, Voice and Loyalty* (1970). Hirschman argues that the market incentives put in place by rivals may be partially-replaced by the consequences of consumer resistance. If people who desire political services are locked into a regime because there is no feasible alternative and for this reason cannot 'exit' from the regime, then an alternative response to a decline in the quality of services provided is to complain, to use their 'voice'. A rational politician responds to voice because it is costly to ignore, according to Hirschman, for two reasons.

First, dissatisfied consumers can impose direct costs on political entrepreneurs. They can do this by various forms of direct and indirect action. Some of these forms of action are individual responses akin to those of dissatisfied consumers – for example taking up politicians' time by writing letters to them that might need to be read and answered, asking awkward questions, making complaints and generally being a stone in the shoe of the shirking politician. Politicians are forced to listen to their clientele in order to get a sense of what the public wants. The vigorous use of voice can impose costs by overloading communications channels that politicians cannot turn their backs on. Other ways of imposing costs on politicians involve collective action – for example strikes, demonstrations, and the like – and thus do raise the issue of resolving secondary collective action problems. These problems may be easier to resolve than others if it appears that the unanimous co-operation of more or less the entire group is needed to sanction some powerful monopolist.

The second reason why voice may be costly for politicians to ignore is that not all consumers may notice a decline in quality, and hence become dissatisfied, at the same time. Those who notice the decline first may, as Hirschman rather plausibly argues, be those most interested in the services concerned and therefore be the most vigilant and most likely to notice the decline. But their complaints may alert other – less sensitive or more apathetic – members of the public to what is going on. Continuing voice may mean that more and more people become aware of the decline in quality, generating still more voice and direct costs for the politician. Politicians may respond to lower levels of voice than might on the face of things seem rational, in order to forestall the emergence of more widespread public dissatisfaction with their performance.

A more significant set of incentives for an incumbent politician, however, derives from the threats to the incumbent posed by actual or anticipated *rival politicians* who would dearly like to win for themselves the contract to supply political services. This contract must by definition be profitable, otherwise the incumbent would not have accepted it in the first place. It will thus be coveted by others who, since the incumbent is not permanently ensconced in office as an absolute monarch, can credibly offer competing proposals to the public in the hope of attracting their patronage. This possibility will force incumbent politicians to shirk less and to deliver political services at a higher level than they otherwise would.

If there is a threat to an incumbent from credible rivals, then there is no longer a guarantee that the incumbent's contract with the public will be renewed when it expires. When the time comes for the contract to be renewed, the reputation of the incumbent in actually fulfilling the promises made in previous contracts will be valuable information for the public, while the availability of rivals will mean that an incumbent with a bad reputation in this regard can be cast aside for a rival who looks a better bet for the future.

Rival politicians, furthermore, have an incentive to expend their own resources on monitoring the performance of the incumbent, identifying shortcomings and drawing these to the attention of the public in the hope that the incumbent's contract will not be renewed. Of course rival politicians have no great incentive, other things being equal, to be strictly truthful, since their main objective is to paint the incumbent in a bad light and take over for themselves the job of providing political services. The interests of rival politicians are certainly not identical to the interests of the public at large.

What they say will need to be taken with a pinch of salt, but they will perform a valuable public role in identifying and shouting about those shortcomings of the incumbent that might merit further public scrutiny. And rival politicians will also have a reputation to establish – if they are to represent a credible challenge to the incumbent – so their allegations about the misdeeds of the incumbent cannot be patently false. For these reasons everyone, including ardent supporters of the incumbent, can benefit from political opposition. It is worth devoting some thought to the manner in which the resources necessary to sustain such opposition can be found.

*Can the group remove politicians who outstay their welcome?*

It can be seen that some of the most important constraints upon incumbent politicians come from the threat of potential rivals. For this threat to be credible, there must be a politically as well as physically realistic possibility of removing even a recalcitrant incumbent from office and replacing this person with a rival. Even if limited powers can be ceded to politicians, we must now confront the 64,000-dollar question of how to remove renegade politicians who outstay their welcome. An absolute monarch can, and presumably will, refuse to leave office since having absolute power means that nobody else can do anything about it. But a political entrepreneur is not an absolute monarch, while still having the power to coerce any individual group member. What happens in such circumstances if a renegade incumbent simply refuses to let go of the reins of office?

When we start to think about this problem it quickly becomes clear that the use we have been making of the word 'contract' is somewhat misleading, since most people understand a contract to be an agreement that carries the force of law. If someone does not do what they said they would do in a contract, then the injured party has recourse to a system of legal enforcement. However, a legal system that allows people to enforce contracts will almost certainly be an important element in the political regime to be provided by incumbent politicians. So we face a classic chicken-and-egg problem. With respect to 'contracts' underpinning the provision of a political regime, there can be no recourse to an independent legal system since the enforcer, the incumbent, will be one of the parties to the agreement. A contract that includes an obligation to maintain a legal system cannot be enforced by the very same legal system to any meaningful extent. In this context, therefore, if an incumbent reneges on the contract and refuses to leave office then what happens is rather more down to earth, resting ultimately on good old-fashioned force.

If an agreement to supply a political regime comes into being, then the incumbents must control sufficient force, as well as having the consent of their clientele, to enforce sanctions on recalcitrant members of the public. This is part of the essence of a political regime that can help resolve collective action problems. Incumbents do not, however, possess sufficient force to coerce the group *en masse*. Collectively, members of the group will as a matter of brute force be able to coerce an incumbent, and thereby remove those who outstay their welcome. Since the incumbent politician must, in order to fulfil the contract in the first place, be able to coerce any individual, forcibly ejecting the incumbent will inevitably require collective action by the group. We must be sure that any second-order collective action problem that arises from trying to evict a renegade incumbent from office can be resolved without recourse to the very regime provided by the incumbent in the first place.

We can return in a little more detail to our western movie to see this second-order collective action problem in operation. Some bad guy has come into town and terrorized the locals, effectively setting himself up by conquest as a Hobbesian absolute monarch. The locals know that, whilst the bad guy is tough and has a gun, they could easily overpower him in a combined assault. They gather outside the bad guy's usual hangout, the local honky-tonk, and tell him to get out of town real fast. He smiles the knowing and sinister smile that got him the part in the first place and shouts back that, although he knows he can't take them all on, he's sure gonna kill the first person who walks through that door. Each of them knows that the bad guy is willing and able to do this and none of them, for this reason, wants to be first through the door. The bad guy drinks on in comfort and the townsfolk's collective action problem continues. The fact that, taken together, they could physically overpower the bad guy is no guarantee that they will, politically, be able to do so. This, it will be remembered, was when the townsfolk sent out for a hired gun.

One intriguing method for producing the collective action needed to remove incumbents who refuse to leave office under the terms of their contracts does indeed arise as a result of competition from rival political entrepreneurs. A rival politician may supply the political services to underwrite the second-order collective action needed to remove a renegade incumbent and may regard this as an investment. This investment would be made for exactly the same reason as the rival invests resources in being an out-of-office rival in the first place – in the expectation of making a subsequent contract with the group to supply political services. Indeed this expectation must now be enhanced by the knowledge that it seems most unlikely that an incumbent who has had to be forcibly evicted from office will be offered another contract to supply political services by the group.

Once more, we see that the possibility of competition from rival political entrepreneurs is very important for the public. Failing such competition, members of the public will only be able to remove an incumbent who refuses to leave office on the basis of collective action organized from within their midst. But the very difficulty of organizing such collective action is the reason the group got involved with the incumbent in the first place. We also see, however, that the potential rewards for a rival politician who underwrites the costs of overthrowing a renegade *ancien régime* are greater than those of a rival politician who merely stays in business of opposition in the hope of some day winning the contract to supply political services. It may not be too difficult for the group to find a rival politician who will indeed be prepared to underwrite the costs of getting rid of a renegade incumbent.

## Sustaining opposition to the incumbent

The benefits provided by rival politicians can for the most part be enjoyed just as much by those members of the public who do not pay for them as by those who do. The benefits of political opposition will therefore also be highly susceptible to free riding. There are at least three ways of addressing this problem.

The first involves opposition politicians promising that if they achieve office they will confer selective benefits on those who sustain them in opposition. One obvious way of doing this would be a patronage system, under which opposition politicians would promise their supporters certain public positions in the event that they became the incumbent. Whatever else might be said about a patronage system, it does provide one way in which political opposition may be sustained on the basis of contributions from people who cherish a reasonable expectation of receiving lucrative public positions if their candidate becomes the incumbent. Supporters of opposition politicians would in effect be investing some of their private resources in the expectation of receiving patronage favours at some time in the future.

The second method of sustaining opposition to the incumbent is that opposition politicians may use their own private resources to keep themselves alive when out of office, without the patronage of the public, because they are making a private investment in the potential benefits of future incumbency. On this account, opposition politicians must be people with real hopes of being future incumbents. No pay off accrues to a rival from being in opposition *per se*, just as competitors in private markets receive no pay off simply for providing the valuable public good of competition with other private producers.

An intriguing paradox arising from viewing rival politicians solely as people making an investment in the future prospect of incumbency is that, if incumbent politicians are perfectly effective at responding to the threats posed by opponents, then opponents will never become incumbents. Once there is no expectation of being an incumbent, however, it is not rational to invest in this possibility; opponents will wither away and the threats that they pose will dissipate.

This in turn implies that rival politicians, as well as their private supporters hoping for future patronage, will only make investments in political opposition, thereby producing competition for the incumbent and benefits for the public at large, if they expect that the incumbent may not match the offers that opposition politicians make to the public. This may be because the incumbent has imperfect information. In a world of imperfect information, politicians do not know the precise private desires of every member of the public. Yet only if they do can they be confident of not making mistakes in their attempt to match the offers of rivals. If the incumbent faces two rivals, for example, offering different deals to the public, then it may not be possible with imperfect information about the preferences of the public to decide which of the two counter-offers it is most important to match. An incumbent may also be unable to match the promises of rivals because of poor past performance in office. Incumbents' promises are almost certain to be evaluated by members of the public in the light of past fulfilment of earlier promises in office. An incumbent's past record in this regard may be poor enough to devalue future promises very seriously and make it effectively impossible to respond to an opponent.

What is important in this context is that the aspirations of rivals to replace the incumbent are quite possibly realistic, so that those rivals do provide incentives for incumbents to honour their contracts with the public.

A third possible way for rival politicians to be financed may seem paradoxical at first sight – they may be supported as part of the political regime provided by an incumbent! The intuition here is that the public will be well aware of the possibility for incumbents to shirk on their deals after they take office, especially given the fact that incumbents will have a lot more information than members of the public about what is actually going on. As part of the process of trying to negotiate with an incumbent, therefore, members of the public may feel much happier if some of the political services that are provided include the services of political opponents who will monitor and challenge the incumbent. While any aspiring incumbent might well prefer to do without an opposition entirely, members of the public have quite the opposite incentives and may be able to insist upon the public financing of rival politicians as part of the political regime that they contract for.

To sum up, the public benefits of political opposition can be provided as follows: by rival politicians themselves as an investment in the possibility of future incumbency; by other people who expect to receive selective private benefits from a future incumbent; or as part of the political regime contracted for by members of the public. If the costs of opposition are sufficiently large to be beyond the reach of most individual aspiring politicians, then the funding of opposition either on the basis of some form of patronage system, or funding it as part of the political regime itself, appear to be the main alternatives.

## The structure of competition between political entrepreneurs

So monopolistic political entrepreneurs may produce some political services in order to avert the damaging consequences of consumer resistance, but it is the threat of competition from rivals which greatly increases incentives to honour the contracts that political entrepreneurs make with the public. The nature of this competition differs quite radically from the nature of competition in the market for private goods and services, because of the very nature of political services. With private goods, competition can take the form of 'simultaneous provision' of similar or identical goods by a number of competing entrepreneurs. Because, by definition, it is possible to exclude people from the consumption of private goods, simultaneous provision presents no problems. Each entrepreneur has a group of clients with whom private goods contracts are made. If any client refuses to meet the obligations of this contract, then he or she can be prevented from consuming the good.

The exclusionary sanctions operated by private entrepreneurs are such that two or more entrepreneurs can operate sanctions simultaneously without necessarily coming into conflict with each other. We have also seen that the objects of people's desires may exhibit a fair degree of 'publicness' yet be such that it is still possible to exclude people from consuming them. An example of this is a park, which is jointly supplied to a group of consumers despite the fact that it is possible to install and police a gate on the park and thereby stop specified people from enjoying it. Once through that gate, however, all consumers have equal access. Entrepreneurs realize a surplus from organizing the supply of such things on the basis of their ability to exclude potential free riders from consumption of benefits towards which they have not contributed. In these cases, simultaneous provision of similar goods by rival entrepreneurs is perfectly possible, since the passive sanctions involved imply no necessary conflict between them. Two or more entrepreneurs could thus set up rival parks or fire brigades simultaneously, and compete with each other on the basis of providing these things only to people prepared to pay for them, while excluding those who are not.

Many of the objects of people's desires, however, are such that it is not economically feasible to exclude specified individuals from consuming them. A political entrepreneur may have a role in facilitating the provision of these 'non-excludable' goods and services, but only on the basis of having the power to coerce free riders. Simultaneous provision of similar political services by rival entrepreneurs then presents severe problems.

These problems arise because, while it is easy to envisage sanctions that can be directed against any individual, it is much harder to imagine sanctions that can be directed only against members of a predetermined group of individuals, such as the clients of a specific political entrepreneur. One possible exception, the logic of which might be generalized, is illustrated by the relationship between a drug dealer and a junkie. The dealer's threat to stop supplying the drug is a sanction which might appear awful to the junkie, but which would leave all who are not junkies absolutely cold. The dealer is an entrepreneur who thus has power only over junkies. If the sanctions at the disposal of rival incumbents cannot be confined to predetermined individuals, however, which is the more typical situation, and if two or more incumbents are simultaneously providing similar or identical services to the same public, then there is the potential for serious conflict.

This arises from the need for political entrepreneurs to deploy sanctions against free riders. The reputational effects we have already considered may provide incentives for incumbents to deal fairly with those they have contracted with, with their own principals in the public at large, using sanctions only when this is provided for in the contract and not otherwise. However, incumbents have no incentive to deal fairly with other members of the public, while they do have the resources to coerce them. Thus they may well attempt to impose sanctions upon the principals of rival incumbents, in an attempt to extract resources from them even when these have not been agreed by the victims. Indeed, it may even be in the interest of an incumbent's existing support base for the principals of rival incumbents to be subjected to such sanctions; any funds that are raised in this way, and any new recruits who are thereby encouraged to join the fold, may reduce the costs borne by those who are already there. Competition between incumbents will be just as likely to involve punishing rivals' supporters as to involve incumbents striving to improve their own performance and offer the public a better deal. When two or more rival incumbents are simultaneously in the field, one will always be thinking that the other's principals are recalcitrant. The incentives for incumbents to improve performance will, furthermore, be reduced by the knowledge that those dissatisfied principals in the public at large who might want to take their custom elsewhere can be forced to pay anyway.

Competition between rival incumbents *simultaneously* providing non-excludable political services on the basis of coercing free riders who do not pay for these will thus place a heavy burden on members of the public. They may be punished whether or not they are free riders, by incumbents of whom they are not a supporter. The incentives for incumbents to improve their performance in the face of competition from rivals will also be diminished. Competition on the basis of simultaneous provision of political services by rival incumbents may well not force incumbents to compete by trying to offer consumers a better deal than their rivals.

An alternative mode of competition for contracts to supply political services is 'sequential monopoly'. Under this arrangement, a fixed-term contract is put out for tender to rival political entrepreneurs and awarded, on an exclusive basis, to the one offering the best deal. When the fixed term expires, the contract is put out for tender once more and the process is repeated. This arrangement encourages the incumbent to honour contractual obligations, for fear of losing the contract when it is up for renewal. Furthermore, it does not involve the costs to each member of the public arising from competitive simultaneous provision. Each member will be subject to a contract with a single incumbent and can expect to be on the receiving end of a single set of sanctions if he or she tries to free-ride. The definition of free-riding, furthermore, will be unambiguous since there will only be a single political regime in place at any given time.

### Payoffs for political entrepreneurs

Political entrepreneurs have hitherto been viewed as entirely instrumental actors, receiving rewards from groups in exchange for producing packages of political services, with no concern at all for their own private feelings about the substance of these services. On this account politicians are in the business solely for the rewards they receive from the group for providing political services, and do not care *intrinsically* about the substantive content of the services they provide. This rules out the possibility that politicians are concerned to promote particular packages of political services for reasons that have to do with their own private preferences. The rewards from public office are assumed to derive from producing, rather than from consuming, political services.

Political entrepreneurs are also individuals with their own private desires, however. They may prefer to produce a package of political services that is closer to the one that they privately prefer than the package that would emerge if they did not get involved in politics. Indeed this may even have been a motivation for their getting involved in the business of producing political services in the first place.

There is no guarantee that the package of political services that has been contracted by the group will be the one that is most preferred by the politician given the job of producing it. This creates a further potential conflict of interest between politician and public. Other things being equal, the politician has an incentive to deviate from the agreed package of political services, in the direction of his or her own private desires.

This is another reason why an incumbent politician may be an imperfect agent of the public. An incumbent may substitute political services that are privately desired for those that have been publicly contracted, and this is in effect another form of shirking. Such shirking does not involve giving short measure on the contract, but doing something that was not what was contracted for. The probability of this increases, the more it is possible to get away with not implementing the precise package of political services that has been agreed. The extent to which a politician can get away with this will depend upon factors that are very similar to those which constrained a politician from simply producing less than had been agreed with the public. Two key factors will be reputation and competition.

Incumbents who want to renew their contract with the public when it expires will need to have developed a reputation for honouring their promises, otherwise it will not be rational for people to take these promises seriously in the future. The impact of the reputational incentives facing incumbents will depend to a considerable degree on the extent to which there are credible opponents waiting in the wings. If there are indeed such credible rivals, then the need for the public to tolerate backsliding on past promises will be reduced, since they do have an alternative. Opponents will furthermore have an incentive to monitor the behaviour of the incumbent for any such backsliding, and to publicize this as widely as they can.

To the extent that there is credible competition from rival politicians, the ability of the incumbent to substitute private desires for public choices will be limited. Notwithstanding this, the ability of anyone, even the most eagle-eyed of rivals, to monitor what an incumbent is doing will inevitably be less than perfect. Rivals may have some incentive, constrained it is true by their desire to develop a truthful reputation of their own, to slant their statements about the behaviour of incumbents for their own private benefit, so that their pronouncements may be somewhat discounted by members of the public at large. These factors will give the incumbent some leeway in substituting his or her own private desires for those of the group as a whole. And this in turn provides a further incentive to become a politician in the first place.

We will return to the motivations of politicians when we discuss the politics of coalition, and will by then have considered longer-term inter-actions that may lead politicians to make promises that are relatively close to their own private desires. To sum up thus far: just as individual members of the public may desire things for either instrumental or intrinsic reasons, political entrepreneurs may promote a particular package of services because they feel, instrumentally, that this package will win them the contract with the public, but they may also have an intrinsic private interest in the substance of the package.

## Alliances of political entrepreneurs: political parties

Political entrepreneurs competing to win contracts to provide political services have incentives to band together into alliances. Such alliances, which we may think of as 'political parties', enable politicians to tender for much larger political services contracts, far beyond the scope of any individual entrepreneur. They also allow politicians to realize benefits that can arise from collusion with others and to gain important strategic advan-tages over their rivals.

For all but the very smallest groups, the scale of activity involved in providing a political regime to resolve collective action problems will be way beyond the resources of a single individual. Both the scale of the required activity, and the diverse range of talents needed to realize this, mean that contracts may need a consortium of politicians to generate the required level of political services. A lone politician will simply not be credible as someone who can produce the political services needed to resolve collective action problems in anything other than very small groups.

Political entrepreneurs who are potential rivals will, furthermore, have two further big incentives to collude. The first incentive arises from restricting the effects of competition. One of the main things that forces a political entrepreneur to produce what has been contracted for, and not to shirk, is the threat of competition. Without rival entrepreneurs competing for the contract to produce political services, even if members of the public discover that the incumbent has been giving short measure or has been fulfilling private desires rather than honouring public promises, there is not much they can do about it as long as the shirking is not so huge as to negate the entire value of the political services supplied. An incumbent therefore has considerable incentives to 'take over' troublesome rivals, offering them a piece of the action as a member of an incumbent team, rather than as outsiders undercutting the incumbent's ability to shirk. Of course the transaction will have to be finely judged on both sides, since the rival politician will be giving up the possibility of future exclusive incumbency for a more certain but less valuable part of the current incumbent's profits. The incumbent will be giving away a certain share of those current profits in exchange for the expected higher probability of winning future contracts that arises from reduced competition. It may well be that no such deal can be done between politicians in such a situation, and that the politicians will continue to compete as separate entities. But, in other circumstances, there may be incentives for politicians to join forces in order to reduce the costs of mutual competition.

A further major incentive for politicians to form ever larger alliances arises from the strategic advantages that can be enjoyed by bigger bargaining units. Politicians forming themselves into alliances to take over the incumbency will need to agree upon how to divide up the rewards of office. Bargaining over the allocation of these may involve the use of threats. Politicians will be able to threaten other members of any putative alliance that, if they are not adequately rewarded for their membership, they will throw their lot in with some rivals. The bargaining power of a particular entrepreneur or consortium will thus be directly related to the number of alternative winning alliances that can be joined.

Such threats will, however, obviously be empty if, after a politician leaves the alliance being threatened, this alliance is still in a position to control the incumbency. Politicians are unlikely to receive rewards from those alliances of which they are not essential members, in the sense of not making any difference to whether or not the alliance can control the incumbency. Similarly, if a politician threatens to leave one alliance, even an alliance of which he or she is an essential member, and join another alliance of which he or she is not an essential member, then this will not cut much ice with the alliance being threatened. Since the politician cannot expect to receive any reward from the alliance he or she is threatening to join, the threat is not very credible. Thus, the most credible threats open to politicians involve threatening alliances of which they are essential members with the possibility that they will leave and join rival alliances of which they are also essential members, and from which they therefore expect to receive a share of the rewards of office. The bargaining power of political entrepreneurs will be related to the number of winning alliances of which they are essential members.

Consider a collection of individual politicians, or evenly matched alliances of politicians, each competing with the others. If two individuals or alliances combine, then they can often more than double the number of coalitions of which they are essential members. The most obvious example of this occurs when three equally matched alliances confront each other. No single alliance controls a majority of coercive resources, but any two do between them. The three are evenly matched and control one third of the bargaining power each. If any two alliances are in coalition then each can threaten the other with the possibility of going into coalition with the third. Any two alliances who combine to form a single, indivisible unit can, however, guarantee complete control of the situation. They control all of the bargaining power because the third has nothing to threaten; it is an essential member of no winning coalition. The two combining alliances between them control two-thirds of the bargaining power before they fuse together into a single bargaining unit. After their fusion they control all of the bargaining power. Since the expected payoffs of those combining increase as a result, such fusions would appear to be quite rational.

It is not, however, necessary for entrepreneurs to fuse into units that are in themselves winning, before they can realize gains from such fusion. Bargaining power can often be increased by forming a unit which still does not control a majority of the coercive resources. For example, if there are five entrepreneurs, each appealing to factions in the population that have equal coercive resources, then each entrepreneur will have one fifth of the total bargaining power. If two of these entrepreneurs combine to form a single indivisible unit, controlling double the coercive resources of each of the others, their bargaining power goes up by more than this.

There are now 24 possible ways of putting together a winning coalition of entrepreneurs, and the new, larger, consortium is essential to half of these. (Any sceptical reader is welcome to list all of the possibilities.) By combining, the two entrepreneurs have increased their aggregate bargaining power from two-fifths to one half of the total, with a commensurate increase in their expectations. This gain in power is at the expense of the others who have not combined. These will, in turn, have incentives to look for other combinations to counteract this.

It can be shown that, for any configuration of bargaining power among alliances, there is very nearly always some combination of alliances that as a result of combining realizes a gain in aggregate bargaining power of the sort we have just discussed (Laver and Underhill, 1982; Laver and Shepsle, 1997 also discuss the bargaining incentives for politicians to band together into larger and larger units). There are also very often combinations that result in a loss of aggregate bargaining power, so it is certainly not true that any fusion between alliances of politicians is likely to be profitable in this sense. In general, however, the enhanced bargaining power of larger alliances of politicians will generally provide further incentives for these to combine, encouraging politicians to fuse into larger and larger units.

Political entrepreneurs thus have at least three types of incentive to form the larger consortia that we might think of as political parties. They need to control sufficient skills and resources to be able to submit realistic tenders for political services contracts to large groups. They will collude to restrict competition if they want to have the opportunity to shirk on their contracts with the public or to substitute their own private desires for those of their clients. And they will want to gain the strategic bargaining advantages derived from by combining into larger units. These incentives provide the political context for the birth and life of political parties.

## Notes

1. In the original *Politics of Private Desires*, I relied heavily in my discussion of political entrepreneurs on the work of Frohlich, Oppenheimer and Young. I am now much less convinced by their argument that political entrepreneurs are people who supply collective consumption goods to the group using a conditionally granted power of taxation, retaining part of the surplus for themselves. Surprisingly little has been written on this topic since Frohlich et al.'s (1971) comprehensive treatment. So I have been forced, in what follows, to make up many of the arguments myself.

2. Thanks and/or apologies are due to my friend and colleague Kenneth A. Shepsle, who coined the memorable phrase 'Congress is a "they" not an "it".'

# 5

# Voting

We have just described a process in which political entrepreneurs, or politicians, form alliances, or political parties, in order to compete more effectively for contracts to supply some bundle of political services that we can think of as a regime. Politicians and/or political parties compete for the approval of a faction, or set of factions, within the population which is in a position to impose its will upon the public as a whole, in the sense that there is not a rival set of factions with both the coercive power and the common purpose to oppose this.

The more nearly equal (or uncertain) the distribution of coercive resources in the population, then the more likely it is that a group that can impose its will upon the rest of the group will also contain (or be assumed to contain) a majority of the population. In this event, any package of political services that is not opposed by a majority of the population is capable of being sustained as the political status quo. The award of a contract to supply such a package may in these circumstances follow a ballot of the population, or election, in which alternative regimes are evaluated by each member of the public. The purpose of the ballot is to identify packages of political services that would indeed be opposed by a majority of the population.

Note that this interpretation of the role of elections differs quite distinctly from many popular conceptions of the purpose of finding out the wishes of a majority, which often lay stress upon the idea that a majority 'chooses' some particular most-preferred outcome from a menu of alternatives, an outcome that can in some sense be regarded as 'the will of the people'. Almost never in the world of politics, however, does decision-making start with a perfectly clean slate, with people choosing one thing over another in a complete political vacuum. Invariably in the real world a set of political arrangements is already in place as the status quo before any decision-making process begins, so that the effective decision to be made is whether or not to replace this status quo with some specific alternative. The purpose of a ballot is then to find out whether there is indeed an alternative that is preferred to the status quo by some majority, as well as being preferred by some majority to other alternatives. (There is no point in replacing the status quo with an alternative, only to discover that a third possibility is preferred by some majority to both.) Majority rule in this sense is not about 'the majority' choosing what it 'most wants', but rather about finding out whether or not there is some majority of people who would prefer to replace the status quo with a specified alternative. If there is not, then the status quo prevails *whether or not a majority of people particularly like it*. It prevails because there is no viable alternative.

Competition between politicians in situations where the balance of coercive resources is very uneven, so that a small minority of people can impose their wishes on the rest of the population, is obviously an interesting and important matter. Unfortunately, however, this has not been the subject of much mainstream work in the general field of rational choice theory. (It is another obvious reason for more thought to be given to the political theory of weapons.) The arguments in the rest of this chapter do unfold within the general, and almost certainly unrealistic, assumption that the balance of coercive forces within the public at large is not grossly uneven, an implicit assumption in all rational choice work on voting and party competition. The remainder of this chapter is thus about competition between politicians who are vying to win support in elections for alternative packages of political services that they are offering to supply to the public as a whole. We can think of those politicians who do indeed find themselves with a contract to supply a political regime to the public as being 'in office' as the incumbent.

Competition between political parties is one of the best-known subjects of the rational choice literature and is characterized by its deference to the seminal contribution made by Anthony Downs in *An Economic Theory of Democracy* (1957), a book that is much cited but these days rarely read. This is of course the mark of a truly important contribution to any discipline, and we should not get too hung up on the fact that many of the arguments now attributed to Downs are actually very different from those to be found in the book itself. In this important sense, *An Economic Theory of Democracy* is a state of mind rather than a text. Its citation with approval is a signal that the author is going to proceed to do things in a certain way.

There is no need for more than the very briefest rehearsal of Downs's argument. The 'economic' theory of party competition is concerned with the interaction between a collection of voters, each trying to maximize personal well-being, and a group of political parties, each trying to maximize the chance of supplying political services to the public. Parties are assumed to be homogeneous coalitions of politicians, and to function as if they were unitary actors. They formulate ideologies, or proposed political regimes, to reduce the cost to voters of collecting and evaluating the vast amount of information necessary to make an optimal voting decision. Ideologies also provide parties with an aura of stability and consistency which, they hope, will increase voters' evaluations of their competence and good faith. Party ideologies in the original Downsian world can be compared with each other by arranging them along a single 'left–right' dimension. In other words, comparing the ideology of any two parties, we would say either that they were identical, or that one was to the left, or to the right, of the other. Individual voters have a set of private desires, which are constructed in such a way that each voter will most prefer some proposed regime that can be described in terms of a particular point on this ideological dimension.

Parties compete by modifying their ideologies, effectively shifting the position of these on the ideological spectrum, in an attempt to appeal to as many voters as possible. Each voter votes for the party whose ideology is at the position closest to his or her most preferred position. The objective of a Downsian party strategist is to set party ideology at a position on the ideological spectrum that maximizes the number of voters who prefer that position to the position being put forward by any other party. This implies optimizing party ideology with reference both to the distribution of views among voters as a whole, and to the ideologies of rival political parties.

Considerable theoretical development has taken place in this general field over the years since the publication of Downs's book, although a number of essential features have been preserved in most of this. Each 'Downsian' theory of party competition begins by making some assumptions about the distribution of tastes in the electorate. Each is based on the assumption that rational voters will, consciously or unconsciously, balance the various programmes of the competing political parties and vote instrumentally for the party that offers them most. Obviously, this means that our under-standing of party competition must be inextricably intertwined with our understanding of why and how people vote. Before going on to look in more detail at party competition in the next chapter I will explore, first, why it might be rational to vote at all and, second, how a voter might cast a rational vote, having eventually made it to the polling booth.

### To vote or not to vote: the paradox that ate rational choice theory

If voting involves some net cost (in the form of information-gathering, decision-making, shoe leather and general mental distress arising from paying attention to election campaigns), then rational voters must expect to get some real benefit from the act of voting before they set out for the polling station. This sets up a problem for rational choice theory that was noted in Downs's original work and has served both to intrigue rational choice theorists and infuriate their critics ever since. The problem concerns why rational people would ever vote at all, given the tiny chance that any one of them has of actually influencing the final result. This has sometimes seemed, as Fiorina (1989) put it so starkly, to be the 'paradox that ate rational choice theory'.

The problem can be very simply stated. The perceived difference between two possible election outcomes may be quite large for many individual voters but, in all but the most tiny of electorates, any one voter is likely to have no more than an almost infinitesimal effect on the eventual outcome. Actually, once we think more carefully about this, the probability of influencing an election result is not as straightforward as it might seem at first sight, given the fact the we may well have some idea about how others might vote, about how they think we might vote, and so on. Large and complicated calculations can be performed on this problem but they will all come to the conclusion that, whatever its precise value, the chance that I, personally, will be the one person whose vote changes the outcome of some national election is really very small. We can also cut the fancy calculations and turn to history, observing that no democratic national election result on record has ever been determined by a single vote. No matter how we look at it – upside down, backwards, or inside out – the probability of any individual voter affecting the result is microscopic. This means that the expected utility of voting, calculated as the value of making a difference in the outcome discounted by the probability of actually doing so, must be really very small. This low expected return is unlikely to justify incurring any realistic level of voting cost.

To put some flesh on these bones, imagine you are voting in a medium-sized country and are choosing between two outcomes, Heaven and Hell – you prefer Heaven. You have about a one in ten million chance of being the one person whose vote makes all the difference to the outcome of any given election. Imagine that the extra cost to you of actually voting was awfully cheap, say ten cents. This means that *Heaven must be worth a million dollars more than Hell* to you, personally, before it is rational for you to go out and vote, which is an activity that amounts to betting ten cents on a ten million to one shot. These don't look like sums that are ever going to add up; voting almost certainly costs more than ten cents, while only the stinking rich are likely to find that the difference between one election result and another – between Heaven and Hell – is anything even vaguely like a million dollars.

This appears to lead to the very awkward conclusion that voting is not rational. Since many people do actually vote, this seems to imply that many people are not rational and thus that a rational choice theory which assumes they are indeed rational is out of touch with reality. This is why the phenomenon of voting in large electorates might seem to point to a paradox that does eat at the very heart of rational choice theory. Furthermore, our ability to solve the problem of why people go to the polling station determines our ability to use assumptions about voter rationality to explain how they actually vote when they get there, and from these to deduce a rational choice theory of party competition. All of this explains why many rational choice theorists have thrown themselves with such vim and vigour into the task of 'solving' the calculus of voting problem by fair means or, it must sometimes sadly be said, by foul.

One obvious way to try and solve the problem of why rational people might vote is to work on the costs and benefits involved and somehow try to make the sums add up. As the rough example used a couple of paragraphs ago should indicate, this is an uphill task.

Consider the costs of voting. Given the tiny probability of affecting the result by voting one way or the other, we might not expect voters to engage in costly deliberations on deciding how to vote. Various methods may be adopted to economize on the costs of deciding how to vote, while still retaining the expectation that a vote will be deployed effectively. Voters may, for example, vote in the same way as other people who they take to be better informed than they are while having the same basic tastes. (We can think of such people as 'opinion leaders'.) People may vote in the same way as their parents, as their friends, as their workmates, or on the basis of any number of other cues and stimuli that they use to reduce the cost of deciding how to use their vote most effectively.

It might also be argued that voting costs in the real world are actually very small. Furthermore political parties, who are interested in winning votes, may help people who they expect to support them in the election by finding ways to reduce their voting costs. We have already seen that Downs presents the development of party ideologies as one method which parties have of reducing voting costs, by making voters' decisions more straightforward. The more complex and incomprehensible the decisions faced by voters, the less likely they are to bother voting. As well as helping voters with their decision costs, parties can also try to reduce the cost of turning out, providing transport to the polling station, child-minding while parents vote, and other help. Voting costs can be driven down in a range of different ways but, as our example shows, even tiny residual costs will be a disincentive to vote, given the minuscule probability of affecting the eventual result. Essentially, voting costs needs to be made as near to zero as makes no difference if this is our chosen means of solving the collective action problem. Short of actually paying those who vote, it is hard to see how this can be done without in effect assuming the problem away. The same essential argument applies to the expected benefits of voting, since these would have to be assumed to be unrealistically large for most ordinary people in order to offset any small residual cost that they may face, and in this way make it rational for them to go out and vote.

A related approach to solving this problem is to assume that voters wildly overestimate their impact on the world and just do not realize quite how small is the probability that their vote will actually change the outcome of an election. I will not devote time to this approach here, since it seems to me simply to be throwing the baby out with the bath water to assume that 'rational' voters will be systematically and massively wrong about one inconvenient fact, despite all evidence to the contrary. If their rational calculus goes so badly wrong in this quite straightforward circumstance, why should we rely upon it to explain anything else?

An alternative approach was first expounded by Downs himself. Downs attempted to deduce real benefits for the individual consequent upon the act of voting by arguing that, if nobody voted, then democracy itself would collapse and all would be worse off. In the language of previous chapters, this argument can be restated as follows. 'If nobody voted, then no threat would be posed to the incumbent, who would then have a massive incentive to shirk on the provision of political services. Everybody would be worse off as a result.' Downs claimed on this basis that voters incur the costs of voting in order to insure themselves against the very high costs they would face if competition were to collapse: 'if voting costs exist, pursuit of short-run rationality can conceivably cause democracy to break down. However improbable this outcome may seem, it is so disastrous that every citizen is willing to bear at least some cost in order to insure himself against it. The more probable it appears, the more cost he is willing to bear' (Downs, 1957: 268).

Our earlier discussion of collective action problems makes it self-evident that this argument simply does not hold water. Competition between politicians, produced by people voting at elections, is clearly susceptible to free riding. Any individual voter can enjoy the benefits of competition between politicians without contributing to this by personally voting. If it is very, very unlikely that any one voter can influence the result of an election, then it is as close as things come in this life to being inconceivable that the vote of any one individual is going to make the difference between the collapse of democracy or not. Thus, voting does not yield any directly consequential increase in well-being from this source, and people will not vote because voting insures them against the collapse of democracy. It will always be rational for any individual voter to stay in bed on election day and let the suckers insure democracy against collapse, for everybody's benefit. The fact that if everyone thinks like this then there are no suckers, and democracy will indeed collapse, does not make this collective action problem different from any other.

A quite different way forward was chosen by Riker and Ordeshook (1973), whose work set the direction for a body of writing, much of which has recently been reviewed by Aldrich (1993) and, in trenchant terms by Green and Shapiro (1994: Ch. 4). Rather than trying to talk down the cost of voting or talk up its perceived effect, Riker and Ordeshook relied upon a number of what they assumed to be 'positive components' in the cost-benefit calculations of voters. These positive components amount to an assumption that, as well as costs, the actual act of voting has benefits for the voter that do not depend upon the outcome of the election. On this approach voters are assumed to derive satisfaction from various things, which include complying with the ethic of voting; affirming allegiance to the political system; affirming a partisan preference; affirming efficacy in the political system; and going to the polls. These satisfactions are neither deduced from *a priori* assumptions nor interpreted in instrumental terms by Riker and Ordeshook, but are introduced as social assumptions in their own right. They all effectively assert that voters enjoy voting for various social reasons, and in this way they undermine the fundamental character of any rational choice explanation of voting.

The assumed satisfaction derived from the act of 'going to the polls' is the most blatant example of this, since we thereby explain the political act of voting simply by saying that people vote because they want to. The assumed satisfactions arising from affirming efficacy in the political system and from affirming allegiance to the political system have very much the same effect.

The assumed satisfaction deriving from affirming a partisan preference was extended by Brennan and Lomaski (1993) into an entire 'rational choice' model of voting based on the notion of 'expressive returns'. The Brennan and Lomaski line is essentially that we observe empirically that rational people do indeed vote, and do take care about how they vote, in the face of clear evidence that, instrumentally, this is most unlikely to make any difference. They conclude that voters must do this for the expressive benefits involved. While Brennan and Lomaski do not use quite the same language as I have in this book, it is hard to escape the conclusion that such expressive benefits are intrinsically valued by the person who receives them, since of their essence they are not instrumentally valued as means to some other intrinsic end.

An example of the sort of thing Brennan and Lomaski have in mind as an expressive benefit can be found in their discussion of why voters who *instrumentally* prefer peace at a time of heightening international tension may nonetheless *expressively* vote for someone who offers them a foreign policy line involving a high probability of war. The reason they do this is alleged to be 'the opportunity to show one's patriotism, one's antipathy to servility, one's strength of national purpose' (1993: 50). These types of motivation are quintessentially social and all of this is of course very far from being a fundamental potential explanation of voting, unless some *instrumental* justification is offered for the desire to show (to others, presumably) one's patriotism, antipathy to servility and strength of national purpose. Absent such a justification for these expressive socially defined benefits, or convincing examples of intrinsic expressive benefits that flow from the social act of voting but are not socially defined, the slick (though logically circular) trick in the Brennan–Lomaski argument is that expressive voting is seen as 'rational' precisely because there is no effective chance of the vote making a difference.

Thus, far from seeing as a problem the issue of why people vote when they know that they can't make a difference, Brennan and Lomaski make a positive virtue of it. If the expressive voter in the previous example were told that her vote did indeed make the difference between war and peace, for example, then her behaviour would be very different. What is clear is that, if we wish to construct a fundamental potential explanation of the act of going to the polls, then we need to provide a private instrumental rationale for the particular types of expressive satisfaction that people get from voting.

The search for such an argument leads us directly to the final satisfaction invoked by Riker and Ordeshook, which is the 'satisfaction of complying with the ethic of voting'. While they do not provide an instrumental justification for the existence of an ethic of voting in a particular group, such a justification could possibly be produced in terms of the arguments developed above. The 'ethic of voting' might be seen as a norm, enforced on the basis of informal social sanctions. People could be nasty to non-voters, could refuse to co-operate with them in other valuable dealings, and so on. In this way, non-voters might incur real private disadvantages as a direct consequence of their decision not to comply with the ethic of voting by going to the polls at election time. Since voting is not so very costly for most people, such sanctions would not need to be very great in order for them to have an effect and make voting rational.

A very important precondition for this norm to be effective, of course, is for non-voters to be identifiable. If the very act of voting is secret, for example if voting is by way of a postal ballot that each voter completes at home, then the norm that people should vote will not influence putative non-voters one little bit. Non-voting can be indulged in with impunity. When the very act of casting a vote is public, however, as it is when people must actually walk into a polling station on a given day, then a norm indicating that people should vote may well provide individuals with sufficient incentive for them to turn out and cast a ballot.

This is no more than one step along the road to solving the problem of why rational people vote. While it might be rational to comply with a voting norm if social sanctions are indeed applied to non-voters, we have not yet suggested a reason why other members of the public would incur costs in punishing those who do not vote. If non-voting is a form of free-riding on the collective benefit of political competition, then sustaining an 'ethic of voting' that deters free riders appears on the face of things to generate second-order collective action problems. If, other things being equal, I want to be nice to you, why would I be nasty to you just because you did not vote?

Einar Overbye (1995) has recently attempted an intriguing solution to this puzzle. As with our discussion of why politicians might honour the promises they make to voters, Overbye's account of voting is built upon the instrumental importance of reputations, coupled with the vital and rather controversial assumption that a reputation built in one area of a person's social life has a bearing upon his or her interactions in other areas.

In a world of imperfect and incomplete information, people's actions in one situation can be interpreted as signals about how they are likely to behave in similar situations. As more and more of their actions are observed over time in many different contexts, people build reputations about how they are likely to behave in range of situations. Essentially Overbye's starting point is that a person has no incentive to have the reputation of operating on the basis of a very narrow and selfish concept of self-interest. This is because people may be very unwilling to trust, or otherwise expose themselves to other reciprocal interactions with, somebody whom they see as being very narrowly self-interested and, more importantly, who uses a very short time horizon against which to evaluate the benefits of future dealings with others.

Put in this way voting is an inexpensive act that could be a worthwhile investment in building the reputation of being somebody who is not narrowly self-interested, who has a long-term interest in successful dealings with others, and whom people for these reasons might want to involve in other, profitable, transactions. Not voting, on this account, sends the opposite signal and might lead to rational ostracization by others who fear that the non-voter may cut and run whenever the opportunity presents itself. Given the rather low costs of voting and its public nature, it is just not worth lying about having voted when such lies may be easily exposed, at considerable cost to one's reputation. Ultimately, according to Overbye, you vote because others will think better of you if you do, and because you can turn this enhanced reputation to your advantage. Others, furthermore, are rational to think better of you for voting, since this shows you investing in a reputation as the sort of person they might in the future want to do business with. While other people do not *explicitly* sanction you for the anti-social act of non-voting, the Overbye argument goes, you do suffer a loss if you fail to vote, if people are inclined to trust you less in their other transactions with you. Putting things in a wider social context, an instrumental concern for reputation in the world outside politics sets up a virtuous circle that leads to rational voting.

The big fly in this ointment is why the act of voting in an election whose result you have no hope of influencing should so conveniently be taken as such a vital positive signal of your reputation in other areas of social life. Why should I not look at you, a non-voter, in quite the opposite terms: 'There's somebody I can do business with – a sensible person who doesn't waste time on the pointless act of voting.' Overbye in effect assumes the contrary, but we need rather more than an assumption if we are to be convinced that this is a reasonable approach to take.

Of course if for some reason the act of voting did indeed function as a rather special social signal in Overbye's sense, then the 'voting as a way to build a reputation' explanation would look quite plausible. But a fundamental potential explanation of the act of voting does need to give some account of why other people feel like this about whether or not you vote. In effect what is needed is to explain why, if you cultivate a reputation as an avid voter, this makes people more likely to lend you money, believe what you say, or otherwise put themselves at your mercy. As yet, such an explanation has not been forthcoming, but this does nonetheless remain a potentially fruitful line of enquiry.

Overall, there have been many different approaches to the problem of why people vote at all, seen as an important precursor to understanding what people do when they actually find themselves inside a polling booth with a ballot paper in their hands. Many of the solutions simply assume away the problem – assuming that people vote because they like it, for example, or because other people punish them for not voting. But our insistence on using fundamental potential explanations of the political realm, explaining social behaviour in terms of asocial assumptions about what fundamentally motivates people, rules out such sleights of hand. What remain are explanations which in effect state that people vote by mistake – clearly unsatisfactory – or that going to the polls is an important expressive or symbolic act, one which can provide individually valued reputational and other benefits for those who vote. The latter approach, for the time being, does seem to be the most promising route towards the solution of a problem that has troubled at least some ordinary decent rational choice theorists for quite a long time now. But this type of solution needs a lot more careful thought if the paradox that still threatens to eat rational choice theory is successfully to be resolved.

## Deciding how to vote

We have just argued that it seems very unlikely that rational people will turn out to vote because they have any realistic hope of influencing the outcome of an election, viewing this outcome in terms of which political party or parties end the day with the job of supplying political services to the public as a whole. We have also argued, however, that it might be rational to turn out and vote for reasons that have rather little to do with the precise outcome of a single election. Assume for the moment that we have solved the problem of why people turn out and vote. Having arrived at the polling station for one reason or another, what does the voter do next?

One possibility is that, having been driven to the polling station by various social pressures and in the knowledge that his or her vote has no measurable effect on the result, the voter simply does not vote – perhaps casting a blank ballot or tearing up the voting paper. But, having got as far as the inside of a polling station, casting a blank ballot would seem to be just as costly an act as casting a valid vote, unless the actual act of completing the ballot is overly long and tedious. In other words, once the voter is inside the polling booth and thereby free from social pressures, the cost of voting relative to not voting is effectively zero. Having got as far as the inside of a polling booth, explicitly insisting on not voting does not appear to be rational. The putative voter might as well go on and use the ballot in a way that has some, albeit tiny, benefit, rather than none.

It is important to remember if we are looking at voting in these terms that voters will not expend *any* significant resources on the decision about which particular way to vote, since such costs can never generate consequent benefits. Voters will therefore use whatever 'free' information they happen to have at their disposal and decide on this basis. It will be up to those with a material interest in influencing the behaviour of voters – notably politicians and political parties – to ensure that information favourable to their own cause is indeed at the disposal of voters.

Many of the potential benefits of voting one way or the other arise from the precise nature of competition between political parties. These benefits depend crucially on differences between the various packages of political services on offer, given that the object of voting is to influence the probability that one or other of these packages will actually be put into practice. These packages may differ from each other in terms of two crucial features. The first relates to the likelihood that the package on offer will actually be enacted. The second concerns the substance of what is on offer. We discuss these differences separately, since the first of them is important even if every member of the public shares the same tastes, while the second only becomes important if there is some diversity of taste among members of the public.

*Will the promised package of political services be delivered?*

If all voters have identical preferences with respect to the packages of political services on offer, then these will be evaluated solely in terms of the extent to which voters believe that successful politicians will actually deliver what they offer. These evaluations have two main elements. The first concerns the likelihood that particular politicians will shirk on the job, either by giving short measure or by substituting their own privately preferred policies for those that they promised. The second concerns the actual ability of particular politicians to deliver what they say they will deliver. Anticipated non-performance by politicians may thus result from intentional malingering, from unintentional inefficiency or from over-confident promises.

These factors in turn depend on the intensity of competition between politicians. We saw that an incumbent who does not face a serious challenge from credible rivals will be inclined to shirk on the job, reaping gains from this either until a credible challenger appears on the scene or until the level of political services being provided is so low that the public at large is effectively provoked into revolution. An interesting consequence of this is that, when there is no diversity of preference in the public at large, people have a strong incentive to vote for opponents of the incumbent. This is either because a particular challenger may credibly promise to shirk less if elected, or because increasing support for the challenger increases the threat to the incumbent and hence encourages the incumbent to shirk less. Thus, when there is no diversity of taste in the public at large, differences in the substance of the policy packages on offer may matter little at elections; voters will instead be concerned that politicians will deliver what they promise, and voting for rivals to the incumbent might seem to be an effective way to keep politicians on their toes.

The relative attractiveness of various packages of political services will also depend on the expected efficiency or productivity of the producer. This will depend partly on estimations of the intrinsic feasibility and coherence of the packages on offer and partly on anticipations of the productive efficiency of those offering them. When discussing an individual's internal decision-making, we argued that some desires (such as walking on water) may be intrinsically unrealizable, while some combinations of desires (such as lying in bed all day and having a perfect physique) will be intrinsically incompatible. Given a limited supply of resources, furthermore, many packages of desires will be in short supply. Voters will obviously evaluate promises made by competing parties in the same terms. They will not believe politicians who promise to walk on water, or who promise to simultaneously give them perfect bodies and allow them to lie in bed all day. Neither will they believe politicians who promise to deliver gigantic levels of political services at next to no cost. Voters will thus have *a priori* criteria against which to evaluate promises made to them by politicians. When a particular group of politicians have been competing for some time, however, voters will also be able to compare the promises made by politicians with their past practice. They will probably be less inclined to believe promises that look like promises which have not been fulfilled in the past. Voters will want explanations of why, given that a promise has previously not been fulfilled, they now have any reason to take it seriously.

The other component of the efficiency of a particular package is the anticipated competence of the producer. Voters may make subjective estimates of this, based on all sorts of information. Especially useful information will be available when the politician concerned is, or has been, an incumbent. Poor previous performance will reduce subjective estimates of competence, while good previous performance will enhance these estimates. This is likely to make an incumbent producing satisfactory levels of public goods appear more attractive than a challenger with no experience. Conversely, an inexperienced challenger may appear more attractive, *faute de mieux*, than a patently unsatisfactory incumbent. This of course provides the major incentive for incumbent politicians to produce efficiently rather than inefficiently, provided that they anticipate some credible challenge at the next election. Once more this provides an incentive, in situations where there is no diversity of taste in the public at large, for voters to vote for opposition politicians. In effect voters send a signal to the incumbent by voting for an opponent in these circumstances – the message being that inefficiency (or shirking) can have damaging consequences. Sending such a message may be at least as valuable to the voter as having some small probability of affecting the result.

*Choosing between different packages of political services*

So far we have been assuming that every person in the public at large has the same tastes with regard to the provision of political services. If there is a diversity of tastes, then the precise nature of the various packages of political services on offer will be a significant component of the decision made by each voter. When different voters have different tastes that lead them to prefer different mixes of political services, then the same package of political services will be valued in a different way by each of them.

The logic of going to the polling station, assuming this to be costly, appears ultimately not to depend upon a voter having a realistic expectation of actually changing an election result. Once the voter is at the polling station those costs have been paid, however, and a voter casting a vote in secret should still behave in such a way as to enhance the prospect of favoured electoral outcomes and reduce the prospect of detested ones.

Decision-making by groups of rational people in such circumstances raises a range of complex issues that have intrigued political scientists for decades. Not least of these is the very clear possibility, when three or more

Table 5.1 *The views of Jack, Jill and Joe-Bob about Ms Brown, Ms Green and Mr White*

|  | Jack | Jill | Joe-Bob |
|---|---|---|---|
| Ist choice | Mr White | Ms Brown | Ms Green |
| 2nd choice | Ms Brown | Ms Green | Mr White |
| 3rd choice | Ms Green | Mr White | Ms Brown |

options are under consideration, that no single option clearly dominates all others as the one 'most preferred' by members of the group taken together. Imagine that three voters – Jack, Jill and Joe-Bob – are choosing between three candidates who are offering themselves at election time – Ms Brown, Ms Green, and Mr White. Jack likes Mr White best; failing Mr White he likes Ms Brown, and least of all he likes Ms Green. Jill, in contrast, puts Mr White at the bottom of her list and Ms Brown at the top, with Ms Green somewhere in the middle. Old Joe-Bob, finally, likes Ms Green best, followed by Mr White and Ms Brown. These preferences are set out in Table 5.1.

What Table 5.1 shows us is that there is no 'natural' winner if candidates are chosen by majority vote. Ms Green beats Mr White by two votes (Jill and Joe-Bob) to one (Jack). Ms Brown beats Ms Green by two votes (Jack and Jill) to one (Joe-Bob). And Mr White beats Ms Brown by two votes (Jack and Joe-Bob) to one (Jill). If they try and choose a candidate by voting then, every time they think they have settled the matter, another vote will replace the candidate just chosen with someone else. There is a 'voting cycle' between the three candidates, and it has no logical end.

In a real sense the choice of a candidate by the three voters is arbitrary. Perhaps they keep voting doggedly until one of the candidates gives up in disgust, after which there will be a clear majority for one of the two left in the race. If Mr White gives up first, for example, then Ms Brown will be chosen by two votes (Jack and Jill) to one (Joe-Bob) in the run-off with Ms Green. Thus if Jill knows that Mr White will give up first, she has an incentive to keep the voting going until this happens. If Ms Green gives up first, then Mr White will be chosen by two votes to one in the run-off with Ms Brown, and so on.

This example shows very clearly that, in a group of people with diverse preferences, there is not just 'a' majority in a given group of voters, but many different majorities, depending upon the precise options up for consideration. This allows for the possibility of voting cycles, in the event of which the outcome is likely to be decided by some arbitrary factor that goes beyond the preferences of group members.

Preferences with the type of pattern described in Table 5.1 have a character that has the effect of creating voting cycles under majority decision-making. Other patterns of preferences within the group will on the other hand yield stable majority choices. If Jack reverses his preference for Ms Green and Ms Brown, for example, neither of them his top choice, then

Ms Green can now beat all other candidates in a majority vote. This is despite the fact that all three people still have a different first-choice candidate. Ms Green wins the day in this example because, even though our three intrepid voters disagree on which candidate they most prefer, one majority of them can agree that Ms Green is better than Mr White, while a (different) majority can agree that Ms Green is better than Ms Brown.

Underlying all of this is the fact that, despite a diversity of tastes among the people involved in the choice, this diversity does have some structure. This structure in turn allows Jack to form the opinion, for example, that his tastes are rather similar to, or quite different from, Jill's. Much of the analysis of voting and party competition that has developed within the rational choice tradition has been based upon one very intuitive and suggestive way of describing potential underlying structures in the diverse tastes of the public at large. The analogy used throughout this work, and for most of the rest of this book, is one of physical distance.

If I think about the views of two other people I can think of one of them as having tastes that are 'closer' to my own than those of the other person. I can think of two people with very divergent tastes as being very 'far apart' in terms of their preferences, and two people with very similar tastes as being quite 'close' to each other. If my tastes change, we can think of my tastes as 'moving' closer to, or further way from, yours.

It is a short step from thinking of differences between tastes in terms of physical distance, and of changes in tastes in terms of movement, to thinking of the structure underlying these differences in terms of some form of 'space' in which both distances and movement can be described. The idea of changes in tastes as movement, in particular, suggests a spatial analogy. Thinking of tastes in this way, the structure underlying the diverse tastes of a group of people can be described in terms of 'dimensions' that span the space. Just as physical dimensions allow us to describe the substance of movement in physical space – telling me whether I am moving north, south, east or west, for example, and thereby distinguishing one type of movement from another – policy dimensions give substance to what we might think of as a 'policy space' used to describe a diverse set of tastes in terms of 'distances' between the preferred policies of different individuals. If two people are moving closer together in their tastes, for example, we might want to know what substantive changes in their tastes are bringing this convergence about.

We need a substantive example to take this any further since, rather like an elephant, a policy dimension is much easier to visualize once you have actually seen one, or at the very least have seen a picture of one. Perhaps the most pervasive of the policy dimensions that people use to describe the structure of people's tastes for political services in modern western societies concerns what has come to be known as the 'left–right' dimension of economic policy. To take a very crude way of looking at this, imagine a society in which wealth was unevenly distributed, together with a set of different policies that have a bearing upon the distribution of wealth. One

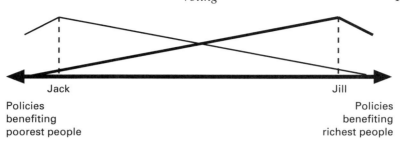

Figure 5.1  *A left–right policy dimension with two voters, Jack and Jill*

policy might be of most benefit to the very wealthiest members of society. Another might be of most benefit to the very poorest. Yet another might most benefit those smack bang in the middle of the wealth distribution. Another again might most benefit those who are poor but not very poor. And so on. There would thus be a series of possible policies, and how you feel about each of these, if you are interested in your own personal well-being, will depend crucially on where you are to be found in the distribution of wealth.

Figure 5.1 shows how two people might feel about a set of different policies that could conceivably be proposed by some aspiring politician. The entire set of possible policies can be arranged according to whether they most benefit the poorest people, the richest people, or some segment of the population between the richest and the poorest. Just for the sake of argument we will put policies most benefiting the poorest people at the left-hand end of this dimension and those most benefiting the richest people at the right-hand end. Policies benefiting those who are neither very rich nor very poor are placed in between these according to the wealth of the type of person they most benefit. These tending to benefit poorer people are placed more to the left. Those tending to benefit richer people are placed more to the right.

Now consider the views of Jack Sprat, a rather poor person, about this range of possible policies. Jack most likes a policy package about a quarter of the way along the policy dimension from the left hand end. The thin sloping line above Jack's name shows the value of each of the possible policies to Jack, and we can see that it reaches a peak over his name. The policy at this point on the scale is the one of most value to Jack, and we can think of this as his 'ideal' policy. The fact that the rather thin line slopes away from this ideal policy shows that Jack values policies less and less, the more these policies benefit people with much more, or much less, wealth than he has. Actually, this line does not need to be straight but for the argument we will be making it does need to slope downwards without ever rising (that is, monotonically) from Jack's ideal policy. Policies to the right of Jack's benefit increasingly rich people, and Jack likes these less and less for this reason. Policies to the left of Jack's ideal benefit people who are increasingly poorer than Jack, and thus also do not commend themselves to him. Jack is in policy heaven if a politician takes office and implements his ideal policy.

We can see that Jill Hornesby-Smythe, a much richer person than Jack, has very different policy preferences for this precise reason. Her views on policy are shown by the fat sloping line above her name. Jill's ideal policy is much further to the right than Jack's; indeed Jill regards Jack's ideal policy as being of very little value to her at all. The ideal policy of any other voter, Ol' Joe-Bob, for example, could also be located on the same dimension generated by this very simple example. The ideal policy would be determined by how the range of possible policies affects the well-being of the individual concerned.

Offered only a series of policies dealing with a single matter, say the distribution of wealth, a rational voter will vote in a way designed to bring about the policy that comes closest to his or her ideal policy, that is, the policy of greatest benefit. This is, in effect, an elaboration of the concept of rational action in the context of voting for one of a range of different policy options.

In a more complex world, people will be interested in all sorts of things, of which the distribution of wealth is but one. Many of these things will be related to each other. Policies bearing upon the distribution of income, for example, will be viewed in similar, but by no means the same, ways as policies relating to the distribution of wealth. Any policy that involves collecting money and producing goods and services will affect the distribution of income and wealth unless by some freak what is produced has benefits for consumers that are in exact proportion to the money collected from each.

All of this could quickly become very complicated. Voters are not likely to spend too much time agonizing about a decision on which they have so little effect. In order to simplify their decision-making, therefore, people may use the fact that many specific policy dimensions are in practice very closely related, and think in terms of bundles of policies that can each be described in terms of some more general underlying 'ideological' dimension. Perhaps the most pervasive of these ideological dimensions is the left–right dimension of economic policy. At the left end of this dimension we find packages of policies that involve high levels of redistribution from rich to poor, high levels of provision of a range of political services financed by high levels of income-related contributions and a general emphasis on collective rather than individual provision. At the right end of the spectrum we find packages of policies that involve redistribution from poor to rich, low levels of provision of political services and a general emphasis on individual rather than collective provision. For a relatively rough-and-ready decision such as voting, this more general ideological dimension may provide voters with sufficient information about the various policy packages on offer for them to be able to make a rational decision about which package to support.

If the preferences of a group of voters can indeed be described in terms of a single dimension of ideology then this, intriguingly, rules out the possibility of voting cycles under majority decision-making. If we go back to our three voters and their views about three candidates, summarized in Table 5.1, then we can see that it is just not possible to describe this set of preferences in terms of a single dimension of taste for different candidates.

As Figure 5.2 shows, we can very easily arrange Joe-Bob's tastes for the candidates along a single dimension. He is 'closer' on this dimension to Ms Green than to Mr White, and 'furthest' from Ms Brown. Thus we now know that Joe-Bob's ideal candidate is somewhere to the left of G\W, the dotted line marking the midpoint between Ms Green and Mr White. If Joe-Bob's ideal candidate was actually located at G\W, then he would not care which of Ms Green and Mr White was elected – he would be *indifferent* between them. Once Joe-Bob's tastes are to the left of G\W this also ensures that he is furthest away from Ms Brown. Joe-Bob's ideal candidate thus lies somewhere in the bracketed area over his name on the dimension of preference for candidates. Jack's preferences can also be described using the same dimension. Jack likes Mr White more than Ms Brown, and thus most prefers candidates to the left of W\B, the dotted line marking the midpoint between Mr White and Ms Brown. Jack also likes Ms Brown more than Ms Green, and this gives us more information about his location – he must be to the right of G\B, the dotted line marking the midpoint between Ms Green and Ms Brown. Jack can thus be found to the left of W\B and to the right of G\B, that is, in the bracketed area over his name in Figure 5.2.

Jill, however, just can't be squeezed into Figure 5.2. She likes Ms Brown better than Mr White, and is thus to the right of W\B. She also likes Ms Green better than Mr White, and thus lies to the left of G\W. But it is just not possible in Figure 5.2 to be at the same time to the right of W\B and the left of G\W. Any point on the line that is closest to Ms Brown must be next closest to Mr White, and this is not how Jill feels about Mr White at all. (It's worth pointing out that this conclusion says nothing special about Jill. We cannot put her on the dimension simply because we have taken her preferences last – we could always find a way to represent the views of the first two people we took from Figure 5.1, but could never squeeze the last one we considered on to the resulting policy dimension.)

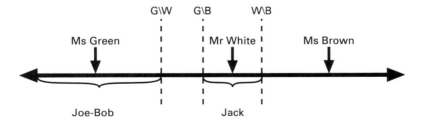

Figure 5.2 *Jack and Joe-Bob's views about the candidates*

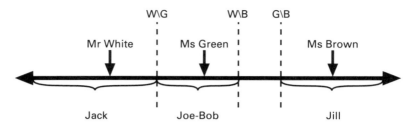

Figure 5.3    *Jack decides he prefers Ms Green to Ms Brown and the voting cycle miraculously disappears*

In fact there is simply no way to arrange the candidates on a single dimension of taste and at the same time satisfy all of the preferences described in Table 5.1. Conversely, if the preferences of members of a group can indeed be described in terms of a single dimension of taste, then there will not be voting cycles in majority decision-making. When only a single dimension of taste is needed to describe the preferences of voters, the ideal policy position of the median voter on this dimension will beat all others. This can be seen for the three candidates example in Figure 5.3, which succeeds in arranging the revised tastes of the three voters along a single dimension of taste, which could even be the left–right dimension described in Figure 5.1, once Jack has reversed his relative preference for Ms Green and Ms Brown.

This arrangement of ideal points, or its mirror image, is the only one that can squeeze the preferences of all three voters on to a single dimension of taste – both possibilities put Joe-Bob in the median position and guarantee that majority voting will deliver his first choice of candidate. Every point to the left of his ideal point will be defeated in a majority vote by his ideal point, by two votes (Jill and Joe-Bob) to one (Jack). Every point to the right of his ideal point will similarly be defeated by two votes (Jack and Joe-Bob) to one (Jill). The logic of this example is general, and shows how the median voter is in a pivotal position when decisions are taken by majority voting and the tastes of voters can be completely described using a single dimension of ideology. This result, originally set out by Hotelling (1929) and elaborated by Downs (1957) and Black (1958), has been of immense subsequent importance in rational choice accounts of voting.

Obviously, by expressing everything on offer in the political system in terms of a single dimension of ideology, such an approach involves making a really dramatic simplification of how each of a group of people might possibly feel about the world. Most people interested in voting and party competition now work with a rather more refined and realistic view of the world that assumes people to be motivated by desires that require more than a single dimension of taste for their adequate description. They consider other independent ideological dimensions, which might for example include social and moral affairs – matters on which tastes can be quite uncorrelated with those for different economic policies – as well as dimensions describing policies in terms of religious, ethnic, linguistic and indeed many other different matters.

The preferences of voters for the three candidates in Table 5.1, for example, can actually be perfectly described in terms of two independent dimensions of taste, as Figure 5.4 shows. As a matter of fact the preferences of three people can always be described in terms of a two-dimensional space; the preferences of four people need at most a three-dimensional space; and, in general, the preferences of $n$ people need at most $(n-1)$ dimensions for their complete description.

Figure 5.4 is one among many possible ways of representing the information about voters' tastes for candidates in Table 5.1. We know that Joe-Bob's ideal candidate is closer to Ms Green than to Mr White, and thus on the Green side of W\G in Figure 5.4. Joe-Bob's ideal candidate is also closer to Mr White than to Mr Brown, and hence on the White side of W\B. This means that his ideal candidate is to be found somewhere in the spotted area in Figure 5.4, which also satisfies the requirement of making his ideal candidate closer to the Ms Green side than Ms Brown, and hence on the

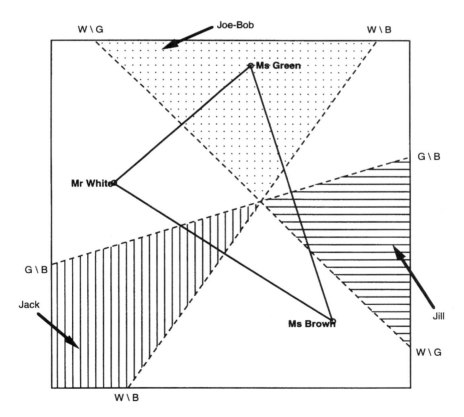

Figure 5.4 *Two dimensions of voters' tastes for candidates*

Green side of G\B. Using the same line of reasoning, Jack can be found in the vertically shaded area, and Jill in the horizontally shaded area – try it and see! All three voters in Table 5.1 can thus have their preferences for candidates represented in the same space, once two dimensions of taste are used to describe these.

The horizontal dimension of this space still looks rather like the left–right dimension we saw in Figure 5.3. The candidates run from Mr White on the left, through Ms Green, to Ms Brown on the right. On balance, as before, Jack looks like the most left-wing voter and Jill the most right-wing, with Joe-Bob somewhere in the middle.

The vertical dimension is new to us, but perhaps it relates to how liberal the candidates are on social and moral issues, with Ms Brown the most liberal candidate, towards the bottom of this dimension, and Ms Green the most conservative, towards the top, and Mr White somewhere in the middle. Jack and Jill both look rather liberal voters, with Ol' Joe-Bob looking distinctly the most conservative – his overall preferences for the candidates rate them in descending order of conservatism, with conservative Ms Green at the top of his list.

The logic of this example generalizes and, if two or more independent dimensions of taste are needed to describe voter preferences, then voting cycles are possible. Indeed, in one of the more important theoretical results in the modern political science literature, it has been shown that voting cycles are very likely indeed when more than one dimension of ideology is important (McKelvey, 1976).

As we shall see in greater detail in the next two chapters, this result implies that the use of additional independent dimensions to describe the intrinsic desires of voters not only complicates the analysis of voting and party competition but fundamentally transforms its conclusions. A very important feature of the preferences of any group of people, therefore, is the set of dimensions of taste that most effectively describes their preferences.

### Collusion between voters: pressure groups

Even though competition for the contract to supply political services may generate a range of rival policy promises, no one policy promise on offer may very much satisfy a particular faction of voters. This raises the possibility that members of such a faction might consider trying to modify the policy promises on offer in order to produce one that they like better. They might do this, for example, by threatening to withhold their support from a particular politician, or even to give it to a rival that they do not much like, in order to try to force the politician they are threatening to put forward a package which more closely corresponds with their private desires.

Such a threat is obviously only effective if it is communicated to the politician concerned, and is very unlikely to be heeded if it is made by a single individual. It does, however, provide an interesting incentive for collusion between voters. If members of a faction of the population share similar preferences which are not reflected in the packages on offer, then they can combine to threaten politicians as a bloc. Threats made by blocs of voters will obviously be much more effective than those made by individuals. Members of a bloc such as this, which we might think of as a 'pressure group', could threaten to withhold their combined support unless changes are made in the policies promised by a particular politician. While this threat, if credible, might indeed induce a politician to modify the policies on offer, we do need to explain how this type of collective action on the part of voters might come to pass, and hence why the threat might be treated as credible.

The first thing to note is that the costs of collective action by the pressure group may not be large. At a minimal level, these involve people in not voting for a politician that they would otherwise have voted for. Especially given the minimal chance of any one vote affecting the result, the opportunity costs of not voting are scarcely huge. There will of course be certain co-ordination costs in communicating with members of the group in order to let them know which strategies have been settled upon. Such costs might conceivably be borne personally by a pressure group leader if there was some directly consequential benefit. Since the views of members of a pressure group are unlikely to be perfectly homogeneous, there is one rather attractive benefit that a pressure group leader may be able to avail of by sole virtue of taking on the role of leader and bearing its costs. This is in focusing the demands of the pressure group very closely on his or her own ideal policy position, an opportunity that would not be available if someone else was leader. Of course, the policy promoted by the pressure group must reflect the preferences of group members, to the extent that the net effect of belonging to the group and abiding by its strategies leaves members better off than they would otherwise be, but only the pressure group leadership is in the privileged position of being able to use the strategic resources of the whole group to advance the fulfilment of their own private desires. Given this, we might expect rather lively competition for the role of leader of particular pressure groups, since these positions offer a potentially effective way to modify the policy promises on offer from politicians at relatively low cost.

# 6

# Party Competition

In previous chapters we painted a picture of politics that shows political parties as alliances of entrepreneurs, competing for the right to supply political services to the public at large. Public demand for these services arises from private desires for things that would otherwise be beset by collective action problems. Rational members of the public motivated by these desires support the politician or political party they judge most likely to maximize their economic well-being. It is almost certain that different people desire different things. In particular, once there is inequality in levels of well-being of members of the public, different people will instrumentally place different values on different packages of political services, some of which, for example, are likely to help poorer rather than richer people, while others are likely to do quite the reverse. This diversity of preferences is likely to have some systematic structure. One way of thinking of this structure is in terms of 'dimensions' of policy or, more generally, of bundles of policies that we might think of as ideology. These dimensions can be used to describe both the range of possible policy packages that can be proposed and the way in which both politicians and members of the public feel about these. All of this describes what we might think of the demand side of political competition. The next step is to turn to the supply side, which is determined by the behaviour of politicians and political parties.

As we saw in Chapter 4, politicians have various sources of utility if they succeed in becoming the incumbents. The first source, and the only one likely to be officially sanctioned by a contract to supply political services to the public at large, is in effect a fee for the supply of those services. The second source of utility derives from a form of shirking that involves putting less effort into the job than had been contracted for. A third source involves another form of shirking, in which politicians implement policies closer to their own private desires than those that they contracted to supply. All of these benefits derive from incumbency. Opposition politicians and their backers, on this account, continue to compete because they are making an investment in potential future benefits of incumbency. A further source of income for opposition politicians may arise if they are seen as part of the wider political regime involving competing politicians, and are thus rewarded for supplying the political service of opposition.

The political incentive structure does, however, reward politicians who get into office. They would prefer their party to be the exclusive incumbent but, failing this, they want to belong to an incumbent alliance of parties. If members of a party anticipate entering into coalition with other parties, then they will want to exert maximum bargaining strength in that coalition. In any case and as always holding all other things constant, the instrumental goals of politicians are best served by maximizing the votes they receive at elections. Increasing their vote increases the chance that their party will gain majority support from voters, as well as enhancing their bargaining strength if majority support is not achieved. The way for politicians to increase their support at elections is to offer a package of political services that as many voters as possible judge to be the one most likely to increase their personal well-being.

Where we go from here depends upon how complex a view we take of the structure of political preferences in the public at large. In what follows, we first take a very simple view, assuming that the structure of these tastes can be represented in terms of a single dimension of ideology. We move on subsequently to look briefly at the implications for political competition if the structure of preferences is more complex, requiring more than one dimension of ideology if we are to describe it in a plausible way.

## One dimension of ideology

Downs's original and immensely influential account of party competition, subsequently elaborated in many different ways, assumed that competition between political parties is structured in terms of proposed policy packages that can be described in relation to a single dimension of ideology. Here, we first consider competition between just two political parties, each free to take any policy position it chooses; this is probably the best-known aspect of Downs's book. We then look at possible constraints on the policy positions taken by parties; at competition between more than two political parties; and at the opportunities for new parties to enter the system.

### *Unconstrained two-party competition*

When just two parties compete for votes and voter preferences can be described in terms of a single dimension of ideology, it is now seen by political scientists as axiomatic that the policy packages offered by the parties will converge on the preferences of the median voter. Notwithstanding popular intuition and the pictures that are often drawn when this conclusion is presented, which show a distribution of electoral opinion in which most voters tend to have preferences towards the centre of the political spectrum, the predicted convergence of parties on the centre in fact holds *whatever the distribution of opinion in the electorate along the single dimension of ideology*, so long as voters always support the party proposing the policy position that is closest to their own.

To see this, look at Figures 6.1 and 6.2. Figure 6.1 shows the typical picture that is drawn of the distribution of preferences in the public at large. On this view, people who prefer policies at the 'extremes' of the policy

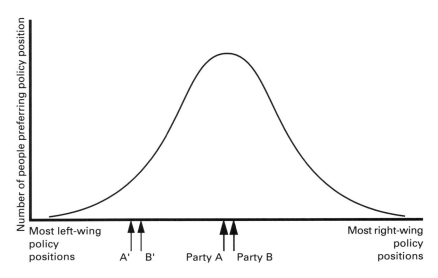

Figure 6.1    *One-dimensional policy competition between two parties*
*with voter preferences concentrated in the centre of the policy spectrum*

spectrum are rather rare, while those who prefer policies in the centre of the
spectrum are rather common. The conclusion that two parties will converge
as they compete with each other upon the policy position preferred by the
median voter seems obvious to most people in this context. Any shift away
from the median position, say a shift by Party A to position A', will make the
party shifting worse off, in the sense that fewer voters will now prefer this
new policy position to the position of the rival party. However, if the rival
party, Party B, tries to capitalize on this shift by taking up a position at B',
then it opens itself up to a response by Party A in returning to its original
median position. (Downs himself assumed that parties cannot 'leapfrog'
each other's policy positions in this way, but this assumption is neither
particularly realistic, nor is it necessary to establish the convergence of
parties on the position of the median voter.) Only when both parties straddle
the position of the median voter is there no policy shift that either can make
to improve its position.

   As Figure 6.2 shows, however, this conclusion does not depend at all
upon voter preferences being concentrated in the centre of the policy
spectrum. The voters in Figure 6.2 can be found in two very distinct groups,
one group comprising people whose preferences concentrate around policies
of the centre-left, another whose preferences concentrate around policies of
the centre-right. Very few people prefer policies at the centre of the
spectrum. However, taking the two groups of voters together as a single
electorate, their views balance out and the median voter does indeed prefer
policies at the centre. Contrary to at least some people's intuition, equilibrium policy positions for the two parties still straddle the policy position
preferred by the median voter, despite the fact that very few voters actually

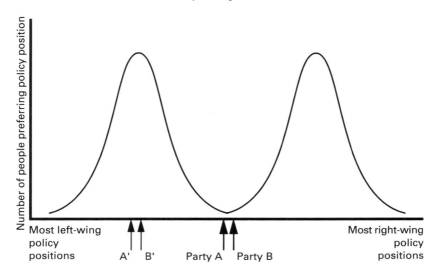

Figure 6.2   *One-dimensional policy competition between two parties with voter preferences concentrated towards the ends of the policy spectrum*

favour this position. The argument about what happens if parties shift away from the median position is precisely the same as it was for the situation in Figure 6.1. If Party A is seduced by the large number of voters who prefer the policy package at A' and shifts policy in this direction, then Party A will lose votes and Party B will gain them simply by staying put. Voters with preferences in between A' and Party B, but closer to Party B, will switch their votes from Party A to Party B. No voter will switch in the opposite direction.

The fact that the equilibrium positions for the two parties remain at the unpopular median position in Figure 6.2 arises, in effect, because every one of the huge body of voters to the left of Party A has no alternative but to vote for Party A as long as it remains to the left of Party B. If Party A shifts further to the left, then left-wing voters will feel happier, of course, but they won't change their votes, because they already supported Party A before it shifted. This gives Party A no incentive to shift in the first place. A precisely similar argument applies to Party B. In effect, both parties can comfortably stay in the centre because voters at the extremes of the spectrum have nowhere else to go.

We should also note that the position of the median voter on a single dimension of policy need by no means be in the 'middle' of that dimension. Figure 6.3 shows a policy dimension in which the distribution of voters is very 'skewed', with many more voters being found towards the right-hand end of the spectrum than are to be found on the left. In this case, the median position will be quite far from the middle of the dimension, but will instead be over on the right. It is on this right-wing median position that the two

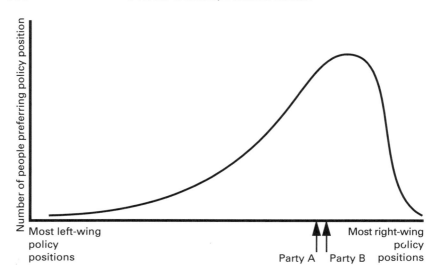

Figure 6.3    *One-dimensional policy competition between two parties with voter preferences skewed towards the right end of the policy spectrum*

parties will now converge. So the distribution of voters on the policy dimension does have a major impact on the outcome of policy competition between the parties, but it does so by determining the position of the median voter, on which both parties converge, rather than by identifying 'popular' positions for the two parties to adopt.

*Constrained two-party competition*

The rather degenerate conclusion that if there are only two political parties in the system they will both home in on the policy position of the median voter and thereby become effectively indistinguishable from one another derives from the assumption that the parties face almost no constraint when deciding which policy positions to promote. It seems likely, however, that a number of factors may constrain their actual choice of policy. These, broadly, have to do with reputation and resources.

When we discussed the logic of voting in the previous chapter, we saw that the act of turning up at the polling booth becomes less likely to be cost-effective, the higher the costs of voting and the lower the benefits. These benefits are determined in part by the (albeit remote) probability of a voter actually changing the outcome of the election. If there is no difference between the policy packages offered by the contenders, then even a voter who expects to have a big impact on the result has no incentive whatsoever to turn out and vote. Thus, as two parties converge on the same policies, the attractiveness of voting will decline. Fewer people will vote because the benefits derived from casting an effective vote become less. This decline in turnout will affect both parties equally and will thus not have an impact on the process of policy convergence.

More plausibly, as we saw, voting may also be seen as a rather cheap investment in developing a rather valuable reputation as a solid citizen. It seems plausible to assume that putative voters will be more interested in developing this reputation among a reference group of 'people like them', with whom they expect to have dealings in the future. In this event, there may be no particular social kudos to be derived from voting in an election in which the only policy offerings are not only indistinguishable, but are also far removed from the tastes of the voter's reference group. If this is the case, then the incentive to vote will decline as the policies on offer diverge from those preferred by members of the voter's reference group. It then ceases to be true, for the electorate in Figure 6.2, that voters on the left have no alternative but to vote for Party A at the median position. They could choose not to vote at all, and this might not damage their reputations *among their reference group* as solid citizens, given the fact that there is nothing attractive for them to vote for. In this event, Party A may have an incentive to move to the left. It would lose a small number of votes to Party B in the centre, but may pick up more votes than it loses in this way from the group of putative non-voters to the left. For a precisely similar argument, Party B may have an incentive to move to the right, rather than to chase Party A leftwards. Differential turnout such as this is probably the type of phenomenon that lies behind the common intuition that a distribution of public opinion like that shown in Figure 6.2 should pull the two parties away from the position of the median voter.

A second set of constraints on the 'degenerate' convergence of two political parties on the ideological centre ground arises because parties have even greater cause to be concerned about their reputations than do voters. After all, politicians compete with each other by making promises to voters at election time, and voters are likely to evaluate both the substance of what they say and how credible the promises appear to be. The past behaviour of politicians will clearly play a big part in voters' evaluations of the credibility of their past and present promises. Voters will be unimpressed with promises, even if the substance of these proposes to do exactly what they want, if they do not expect the promises to be carried out, in effect if they do not regard the person making the promises as credible.

In the abstract sense, of course, it is possible for a politician to promise completely different, indeed quite contradictory, things at different elections, and nonetheless dispassionately and effectively to carry out each set of promises to the letter. Entrepreneurs in the economic market, after all, may develop a reputation for delivering the goods, whatever those goods might be, and whatever their own private desires in relation to the goods produced. Thus cigarette manufacturers may not smoke, whisky distillers may not drink alcohol, drug dealers may not take heroin. An additional complication for political entrepreneurs, as we saw in Chapter 4, is that they have very considerable scope to shirk on the job, quite possibly without being detected, and that voters know that one important way politicians may tend to shirk is by substituting policies that they themselves prefer for policies that they promised at the previous election. This may make voters more inclined to give credibility to a politician who promises to enact policies that are close to his or her own private desires. Such a politician has no incentive to shirk on the job if elected, by enacting policies that differ from those that were promised.

If politicians promise radically different things at different elections, however, they signal either that their promises bear no relation whatsoever to their own private desires, or that those private desires are liable to change radically from time to time. In either event this reduces the voter's confidence that the politician, given the opportunity to shirk, will actually do what was promised. Thus, changing policies from election to election has a cost for a politician, denominated in lost credibility. (This is quite apart from any cost arising from the increased need for resources to publicize any policy shift.) For this reason, the process of ideological convergence may be constrained by a fear on the part of politicians that, if they shift their professed policy positions towards the centre ground in search of votes, then this new policy position may become less credible than their original position by simple virtue of the fact that it has changed. The net result may be that a politician fears losing more votes as a result of declining credibility than are gained by changing policy to a more popular position.

A further set of constraints on party policy positions has to do with an aspect of the internal politics of political parties that we have not yet discussed. We have already seen that parties have incentives to help voters reduce their decision costs. One way to do this is to make clear and simple messages widely available to all voters, something that costs resources. These resources may be denominated in hard cash needed to pay the bills, or the human beings needed to stuff envelopes or take the party message from door to door. Either way, parties with more campaign resources may win more votes. In all but the very smallest of societies, the volume of resources needed may exceed those available personally to a politician investing privately in the potential benefits of incumbency. These resources must be found somewhere, and it is quite possible that the flow of campaign resources will be related to the policy position put forward by the party soliciting them. This could well pull party policies away from the median position

Hirschman (1970) and Robertson (1976), among others, have produced a number of arguments on this matter. Both discussed the consequences of ways in which resources are made available to parties, Hirschman concentrating on party workers and Robertson on financial sponsorship. Both show that, if a party's ability to attract these resources affects its ability to win votes, and if its policies affect its ability to attract resources, then its optimal policy position is not necessarily the one which is most popular with the electorate. Each party will then need to trade off its appeal to the electorate against its ability, in terms of resources, to transform this appeal into actual votes.

Those who contribute campaign resources to political parties must do so for some purpose. This purpose must be to influence the package of political services that is eventually implemented after the election. An individual contributor of resources, whether this is someone who contributes cash or their own labour, must do so in an attempt to bring the package of political services that is eventually implemented closer to the one he or she most prefers. In very general terms, therefore, we can see that such contributed resources must be intended to shift the policy equilibrium away from that which it would otherwise have been. If the policy distribution of available campaign resources does not perfectly match the distribution of preferences in the electorate, as this implies, then this process may well disturb the policy equilibrium under which both parties converge on the median voter. Party policies may be pulled in the direction in which campaign resources become increasingly available, and there is no reason whatsoever to suppose that this is the centre of the political spectrum.

Take the distribution of opinion in the electorate shown in Figure 6.2, for example and assume, plausibly enough, that the main potential contributors of campaign resources have preferences close to one or other of the twin peaks of public opinion. Perhaps, for example, the main sources of campaign resources are the types of pressure group that we discussed at the end of Chapter 5 and there is one main pressure group co-ordinating the actions of each of the two main sub-populations in the electorate. In this event, campaign resources flowing to Party A, whether these are financial or human, may increase as Party A moves towards the leftish peak of public opinion. The leftish pressure group may indeed strategically structure the flow of campaign resources it makes available so as to achieve this. As a result, Party A's ability to win actual as opposed to potential votes may increase as it moves away from the median. Similar forces could pull Party B in the opposite direction.

There are certainly other factors that have an impact on the general conclusion that two parties competing on a single dimension will converge on the position of the median voter. However, the reputational and resource effects we have just discussed combine to produce a fairly plausible account of why, even when there are only two parties, these may not invariably end up promoting centrist policy packages that are effectively indistinguishable from one another.

*Multi-party competition*

Comparing two-party and multi-party competition for votes in the electorate, the most obvious difference is that competition between two parties is effectively zero sum – one party's gains will be entirely at the expense of the other. When there are more than two parties, this is not the case. Two or more parties may each gain at the expense of others, or may lose votes together; they may therefore have common, as well as conflicting, interests.

Associated with this, when more than two parties contest the election, is the possibility that no single party will achieve a majority. It may be necessary, after the election, for the parties to form alliances in order to be able to take over the position of incumbent. Alliances of parties will be discussed in much greater detail in the next chapter, but it is worth noting at this point that the ability of a party to get into office in such cases may well depend upon its policy positions as well as its voting strength. Parties must therefore consider the effects of their policies on their ability to do deals with other parties as well as on their basic electoral popularity. Vote-maximizing policy positions may not necessarily maximize a party's chances of getting into power. A particular change in policy could lose votes but put the party in a superior bargaining position.

As with the two-party case, if we do not consider any constraint on the ability and willingness of parties to set policy positions, then we can derive various equilibrium multi-party configurations of parties on the single ideological dimension under consideration. These derivations can be quite complex and vary under different assumptions – thinking in this area has advanced very considerably on Downs's original discussion of the matter. This work is expertly and rigorously summarized in Shepsle (1991), which should be consulted by readers interested in finding out about equilibrium configurations of one-dimensional multi-party systems under various assumptions. One intriguing result that runs through most of these policy configurations is that three-party systems tend to have no equilibrium policy configuration, leading to the supposition that such systems will be inherently unstable.

In the remainder of this section, however, I concentrate upon what is distinctive about multi-party electoral competition: the potential for collusion between political parties. If two parties have ideological positions that are adjacent to one another, for example, and if each party faces competition from another on its opposite ideological flank, then it may be rational for the two parties to agree, implicitly or explicitly, not to converge on one another when they would otherwise face incentives to do so. The parties will each do better to keep their distance, rather than converging and there by losing votes to the rivals on their opposite flanks. This can be seen from Figure 6.4, a modification of the example in Figure 6.1.

Figure 6.4 shows possible policy positions for four parties: A, B, C and D. Assume, just to keep the argument reasonably simple, that the positions of Parties A and D are constrained by factors that need not concern us here – their position in relation to differential turnout and resource flows, for example, competition with more extreme parties, or any number of other possible constraints. Parties B and C might eye each other and wonder what to do. After all, if Party B were to begin to move towards the centre, then it would enjoy a net gain of votes. Given the distribution of electoral preferences shown, with the density of votes increasing towards the centre of

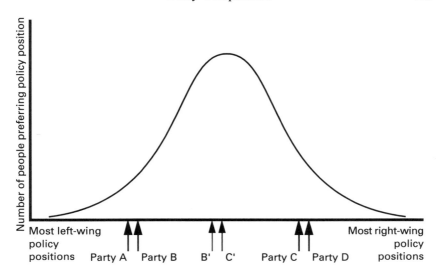

Figure 6.4 *The potential for collusion in one-dimensional policy competition between four parties*

the policy spectrum, more votes would be won from Party C than would be lost to Party A if Party B moved towards the centre. Party C faces an identical situation. If both parties move steadily towards the centre they may end up straddling the median voter at positions B' and C'. Both will be worse off than before they started to move. At the end of it all, Party B now takes only a share of the vote located between B and B', whereas at the start of the process Party B took it all. Similarly, Party C now has to share the vote between C and C', whereas before it took it all. Furthermore neither party has a unilateral move which improves this position. If Party B tries to move back to the left from B', the net result is a loss of votes to Party C.

But what if, before any move is made from their original positions, Parties B and C anticipate the consequences of this mutually destructive competition, which ultimately serves only to increase the vote shares of their rivals, Parties A and D? They might then tacitly or even explicitly collude, neither moving towards the centre despite the short-term attractions of doing so, provided the other reciprocates. The two parties can thus be seen to be playing a game with each other akin to the repeat-play Prisoner's Dilemma game discussed in Chapter 3; their collusion can thus be seen as a pair of conditionally co-operative strategies designed to 'solve' this game.

In general terms, therefore, the types of incentive illustrated by this example mean that electoral collusion between parties is likely to involve the colluding parties keeping their distance ideologically, and agreeing at least implicitly not to compete over the ideological gap between them. This prevents the potential loss of votes to third and fourth parties that would arise if the colluding parties did indeed compete. For this reason, almost paradoxically, electoral collusion is unlikely to result in the convergence of party policy. Thus, to the extent that the parties in a multi-party system do collude in either an explicit or a tacit manner, the tendency for ideological convergence on the median voter may be reduced.

This will particularly affect ideological convergence in the centre of the spectrum, since the parties at either end of it will have nothing to gain from making such deals. The leftmost and rightmost parties should not collude with their ideological neighbours, since they lose no votes by entering into ruthless ideological competition with them. Thus, while ideological collusion between parties may stop convergence on the centre ground, it should leave competition at the extremes of the policy spectrum as intense as ever.

In contrast to this, anticipation of post-electoral bargaining may make parties want to converge ideologically. Here we face something of a logical chicken-and-egg problem. Competition between parties takes place both during elections, in the competition for votes, and after elections, in competition and co-operation between parties to take over the incumbency, given the vote shares that they have won. The two forms of competition interact, and we cannot analyse one without analysing the other. But we have to start somewhere. I have chosen here to start with electoral competition, and discuss competition over the incumbency in the next chapter. This, however, has the consequence that we now need to anticipate some of the discussion of the next chapter before we can make further progress.

When no party wins a majority of votes, control over the incumbency will depend upon coalitions between parties. Coalitions may tend to form, as we shall see, between parties with relatively similar policy positions. One of the main reasons for this is that, if parties deviate as a result of coalition bargaining from the policies they promised at one election, then their reputations will suffer and they will as a direct consequence be less attractive to voters at subsequent elections. In short, parties will be liable to lose votes if they do not put into practice, when given the chance to do so as a member of an incumbent coalition, the policy packages that they promised their supporters. This is because these supporters will evaluate the credibility of future promises at least partly on the basis of past performance in office.

The anticipation of post-electoral coalition bargaining will in this way feed back into ideological position-taking during elections. This recursive process is extremely complex to model, and success in doing so is one of the big intellectual prizes in political science (for rigorous formal attempts to do this, see Austen-Smith and Banks, 1988; Schofield, 1993; for a more informal discussion see Laver, 1989). As a general principle, however, we can suppose that political parties will be unwilling to promise voters policy packages that they will subsequently be forced to abandon in order to bargain their way into power. For this reason it makes sense for parties to anticipate the post-electoral coalitions that are likely to form and take account of these when constructing their electoral policy packages. In certain circumstances, therefore, parties may put forward packages that are closer to those of some of their rivals than would otherwise be the case, because these rivals are seen as potential coalition partners. This process will not be confined to the centre of the policy spectrum, since all parties that want to get into power will be prepared to make compromises in order to do so.

The effects of parties anticipating likely post-electoral coalitions will, however, be more predictable at the extremes of the policy spectrum than at the centre. Parties at the extremes can only make their compromises in one direction, towards the centre. In the centre of the policy spectrum the situation will be much less clear-cut, although smaller centre parties may tend to converge on their larger rivals, since these are more likely than others to be members of winning coalitions.

In conclusion, the existence of three or more competing parties will create a potential for co-operation as well as conflict, even in a highly competitive party system. At least tacit electoral collusion may be mutually beneficial to groups of parties, although such groups will not include parties at the extremes of the ideological scale. Such collusion will tend to counteract the tendency for convergence on a single, vote-maximizing policy. Parties may also want to set their electoral policy positions in anticipation of potential post-electoral coalitions. Parties at the extremes of the spectrum will have a particular incentive to do this, and their policies may consequently tend to move towards the centre of the policy scale. Thus the equivalent of two-party convergence on a single, vote-maximizing policy is a tendency for the range of policies advocated in a multi-party system to contract at either extreme of the scale, since parties at each end always have an incentive to move towards their closest rivals.

*The entry of new political parties*

I have so far been assuming, albeit implicitly, that it is not possible for new parties to enter the fray, that we can in effect take the collection of political parties competing with each other as being given. This simplifies the discussion hugely but is clearly unwarranted – if it is attractive for existing parties to take over the incumbency, it should also be attractive for putative new parties. Once we allow for the possibility of new parties joining the competition for votes, then we not only have to consider what these potential new entrants might do, we also have to take account of the fact that the very possibility of entry will influence the parties that are already in the system.

New parties will obviously only fight elections if they expect to benefit from doing so. In terms of our discussion up to this point, they must thus have an expectation of enjoying the fruits of incumbency at some stage in the future, either by winning an electoral majority outright or by belonging to an incumbent coalition. (As we shall shortly see, however, there may be other justifications for actual or threatened entry.) This means that the decision of a putative new party to enter the fray will depend upon three things: the costs of entry; the probability of success; and the benefits of such success if it is achieved.

The costs of entry into the political market will depend on a number of things, and can crudely be divided into once-off 'break-in' costs, and recurrent costs of continuing to compete once break-in has been achieved. Non-recurrent break-in costs have to do with the need for a new entrant to make its presence felt as a viable contender, and to launch the policy package it is promising to potential supporters. We can think of such costs, in general, as arising from the need to invest in a new party organization and from the need for higher levels of launch advertising and promotion than will be required in steady state. Such costs load the dice in favour of existing parties, who do not have to bear them. Obviously, the costs of a viable break-in to party competition vary considerably from system to system, depending on the cost and effectiveness of various communications media, the costs of running an organization and so on. The higher the break-in costs for a fixed expected benefit, the less attractive will the contest appear to a new party. This will lower the probability of new entrants and reduce the threat to established parties. To the extent that the established parties can increase break-in costs – for example by increasing the price of various communications media or reducing their availability to new entrants – they have a strategic interest in doing so.

Recurrent costs of party competition arise from the need to maintain a party organization and to contest periodic elections. Obviously, the higher the level of organizational and campaign resources required for a given probability of success, the less attractive entry becomes. These requirements will in part depend on the level of resources deployed by the other parties. The more other parties are spending, the more, other things being equal, a new entrant may expect to have to spend in order to compete successfully against them. In a more competitive party system, existing parties may deploy higher levels of organizational and campaign resources than in a less competitive system, perhaps one in which the parties are effectively colluding. In a close analogy with economic markets, this will make entry into a competitive system more expensive, and hence less attractive, than entry into an uncompetitive system. Conversely, the threat of new parties may well reduce the desire of existing parties to collude and effectively invite entry. The impact of high anticipated organizational and campaign costs on deterring entry might even mean that existing parties choose strategically to keep costs high so as to frighten off new entrants, or even to force poorer existing competitors to exit from party competition.

The probability of successful entry by a new party will also depend on the nature of the ideological 'gaps in the market', policy packages that are not currently on offer to voters, as well as on the precise voting system that is used.

Both the size and the position of gaps in the market will be important. The size of any gaps will obviously depend on the number of parties in the system and on the policy packages they are offering. Other things being equal, the size of the largest pool of voters who would prefer some particular alternative policy package to any package that is currently on offer will determine the likelihood of a successful new entry. The more policy packages on offer, the smaller this pool is likely to be and the lower the probability of success for a new entrant. For a given entry cost, therefore, the likelihood of a new party entering the fray will increase as the number of existing parties decreases. The more parties already competing, the less likely a new entry.

The nature of the policy packages offered by the existing parties will also have a very important effect on this process. This complex matter is reviewed in some detail by Shepsle (1991). Briefly, for a given distribution of electoral preference, the more diverse the policy packages offered by existing parties, the smaller the pools of voters preferring alternatives and the less attractive entry, assuming otherwise fixed costs and benefits.

Figure 6.5, a modification of Figure 6.4, shows this quite clearly. It compares two possible party systems for a given distribution of electoral opinion.

The higher of the two horizontal lines shows the positions of four parties – A, B, C and D – assuming once more, to keep things simple, that the positions of A and D are constrained by a range of factors that we do not consider here. If the number of parties in the system is given, then this implies that parties B and C will take up positions as shown, sharing the pool of voters between A and D. This leaves a large gap in the middle of the ideological spectrum, one that might look quite enticing to a potential new

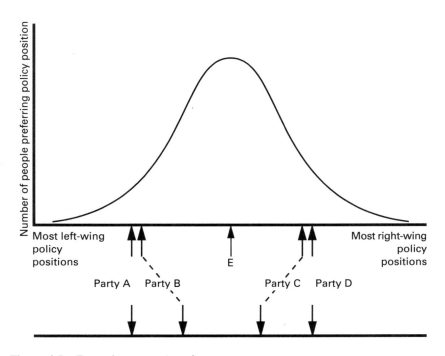

Figure 6.5  *Entry deterrence in a four-party system*

entrant. Imagine that break-in costs, recurrent costs, and other factors affecting entry were such that an entry at E did indeed appear to be cost-effective for some hopeful new party. Parties B and C know this, and they may be able to modify their positions to anticipate and deter such an entrant. The costs of entry may be such that, if both B and C move towards the centre, perhaps to the positions shown in the lower party system (and remember that they may be able to collude implicitly to do this), then the reduced expected benefits arising from the smaller pool of available voters may now make entry non-viable.

Obviously, we need to have an awful lot of information about the costs and benefits we have been so glibly talking about before we can analyse the potential for deterring entry in a particular case, but this example does illustrate a number of general points. First, if entry is completely free, then it is unlikely to be deterred – E in this case might be saddened at the reduced pool of voters in the lower party system, but would be happy to poach these nonetheless. Second, if entry does have costs, which is of course far the more plausible assumption, then it may be possible for existing competitors to act strategically in a way to deter entry by making the anticipated benefits of entry not worth the costs. They may do this by raising entry costs if they can, but they may also do it by acting strategically to narrow gaps in the market. Third, note that narrowing gaps in the market is good for voters, in the sense that more voters are likely to have a party advocating a policy package closer to their own private desires as a consequence. Thus voters may have an interest in keeping entry costs low, since this keeps the threat of entry high and forces parties to respond by narrowing gaps in the market.

A final point to note is that the threat of entry may impinge disproportionately on parties at the ends of the ideological spectrum. For a given gap in the market, an intervention in the middle of the spectrum will poach votes from parties on either side of the intervening party – from Parties B and C in Figure 6.5. An intervention at the end of the spectrum takes votes exclusively from the party that was previously at the end. Thus, in Figure 6.5, if entry costs justify intervening for a pool of votes of a particular size, then Parties A and D have more to fear from an intervention, since they pay the whole price of this, than Parties B and C. In this case, if Party A were to shift left to head off an intervention on its left flank, then Party B, intriguingly, would be the main beneficiary of the entry threat. The threat of entry should thus put greater strategic pressure on parties at the current extremes of the spectrum. This may act as a constraint, if entry costs are low enough, on the tendency of such parties to converge on the centre and may thereby ensure that the overall range of policy positions on offer is wider than it otherwise would be.

Before closing our discussion of entry, we should briefly consider two further matters. The first has to do with methods of counting votes at elections, the second with the possibility of ideologically motivated entry threats.

Different systems of counting votes affect the way in which potential support is transformed into actual electoral representation. Voting systems that are very proportional convert potential support into electoral success more effectively, especially for small parties, than systems that are not. Since, for a given entry cost and ideological configuration, anticipated electoral success will affect the probability of entry, proportional electoral systems will yield higher probabilities of electoral success and therefore increase the probability of entry. Since the probability of entry, as we have just seen, affects the nature of ideological competition between existing parties, proportional electoral systems will tend to have the same effect as low entry costs. The more proportional the electoral system, the greater should be the diversity of the policy packages on offer. Less proportional systems will tend to have the opposite effect, generally restricting ideological diversity.

As a postscript to this discussion, we should consider a type of entry which is not intended to capture the incumbency, but which does flow directly from some of our earlier discussions. Entry and the threat of entry have the effect of modifying the policy packages proposed by existing parties. There may be many people, voters and particularly pressure groups, who would like very much to modify the policies of existing political parties. Actual or threatened entry offers them one obvious way to attempt this. Entry may thus be threatened or enacted precisely to achieve this effect, even if those involved have no chance of capturing the incumbency.

Imagine a pressure group of voters, all with ideal policy positions to the left of Party A in Figure 6.5. They may attempt to move Party A policy to the left by threatening to enter party politics at a position to the left of Party A. Even if the putative entrant has no hope whatsoever of incumbency, this may not be a deterrent. In effect, the entry threat would encourage Party A to move left. Party A politicians might respond by dismissing the threat as not credible and challenge the threatener to do it anyway but, if the new party does indeed intervene, then Party A will be the one that suffers. Who is to say who will win this strategic stand-off between Party A and the putative new entrant? Party A might respond to the threat to move leftwards. Or, if Party A does not move, then the pressure group might indeed enter the fray, with a view to forcing Party A leftwards at the next election.

The possibility of 'ideological' entry by people and groups interested in shifting eventual policy outputs in the direction of their own ideal points raises some very fundamental issues in relation to the motivations of those who compete in party politics. What has been sketched in the above example is a justification for competing that is entirely concerned with the eventual policy outputs of the incumbency, rather than with the personal benefits flowing to politicians who become incumbents. This raises the clear possibility that some of the actors in a party system are there to achieve policy objectives rather than to get into office on the basis of policy promises. In short, those competing at elections might be divided into those who are 'office-seeking', the political entrepreneurs with whom we have for the most part been dealing up until now, and those who are 'policy-seeking' – competing so as to increase the likelihood of the eventual fulfilment of certain private desires. While rational choice theorists have certainly made the distinction between the two types of actor the detailed justifications for, and implications of, this distinction have yet to be developed to any significant extent in a model of electoral competition between political parties.

It should be clear even from this little taste of what might be on offer that the actual or anticipated entry of new parties raises deep and complex possibilities in the analysis of party competition – and we haven't even begun to consider how potential new entrants might behave strategically in order to deter still further entrants! Almost any way we look at it, however, the threat of entry, made feasible by the existence of low enough entry costs to make entry feasible, will have an impact on the existing party system and will almost certainly cause more dispersion of party policy positions than would otherwise be the case.

## More than one dimension of ideology

Even though fascinating but quite difficult issues are raised by thinking about party competition when only a single dimension of ideology structures the preferences of the public at large, it is obviously a huge over-simplification to assume that a just single dimension of ideology can capture any realistic political interaction. It is quite possible for a group of people to have preferences that just cannot be structured in terms of a single dimension of ideology.

Consider, for example, the 'left–right' dimension that we have been talking about up to now. This might be thought of as comprising a bundle of issues on which people's preferences are very highly correlated. Holding capital assets in public ownership on the one hand, and providing high levels of collective consumption funded by high levels of taxation on the other, for example, have to do with conceptually quite different aspects of public policy. Yet, people's preferences on the two matters may in practice be very highly correlated. In other words, in the real world people who favour high levels of public ownership may also in practice tend to favour high levels of public services, while people who oppose one policy may typically oppose the other. If we arrange members of the public along a policy dimension relating to each issue, then the two issues may arrange everybody in the same way. In this case, we can think of policies on the two issues as being related to a single underlying dimension of ideology. While we can talk in theory of two conceptually distinct issue dimensions, real world correlations between people's positions on these mean that in practice both can be seen as aspects of a single more general dimension.

There may well be other issues, however, such that it is quite impossible to predict a person's attitude on one issue from his or her position on the other. Consider attitudes to public ownership, for example, and attitudes to abortion. Just as for economic policy, we can think of a whole spectrum of possible views about the proper role of a group of people in relation to the unwanted pregnancy of one of the group's members. At one end of the spectrum we might think of a 'liberal' position that sees an unwanted pregnancy as being entirely a personal matter for the woman concerned and thus sees the issue of abortion as a private choice made by a woman about her own bodily integrity, something in which the group has no right whatsoever to interfere. At the other end of the spectrum we might think of a 'conservative' position that sees an 'unborn' human being as coming into existence at the moment of fertilization of a human ovum, becoming at that moment an individual quite distinct from the mother, with a right to life that is entitled to the full protection of the group quite regardless of the wishes of the mother. Such people may see abortion as a very public matter.

For our purposes, what is important is that, in the real world, it may be almost impossible to predict how somebody feels about abortion from how they feel about the public ownership of assets. One person may simultaneously favour low levels of public ownership and a liberal policy on abortion, another may favour low levels of public ownership and a conservative policy on abortion. If this was a general pattern, then there would certainly not be a high correlation between attitudes to public ownership and attitudes to abortion. We can think of this as being because each issue is related to a different underlying dimension of ideology. Just as various economic policy issues may all be related to some underlying dimension, so various attitudes to female fertility – to contraception, to test tube babies and to surrogate motherhood, for example – may all in practice tend to be interrelated. They may also be related to attitudes to other 'moral' matters, such as euthanasia, pornography, prostitution or the taking of illegal drugs.

Imagine for the moment that the preferences of the public at large on all salient matters are structured by just two underlying ideological dimensions – in other words, attitudes on any salient matter are highly correlated to one or the other of these underlying dimensions. I will develop the discussion of 'multidimensional' party competition on this basis because this is simpler and more convenient, not least because I have access only to two-dimensional pages on which to draw pictures of what is going on. The basic ideas, however, generalize to any number of independent ideological dimensions that might be important. Imagine, to put labels on these dimensions, that the first relates to economic policy and the second to policy on 'moral' issues. The type of one-dimensional analysis we have been discussing thus far can be embedded in this more general description, as can be seen from Figure 6.6. This shows the same four parties, A, B, C and D, located on the left–right economic policy dimension. This dimension is now, however, seen as being part of a more general two-dimensional ideological 'space', defined by positions on both economic and moral policy. Party positions on economic policy are shown as positions on the horizontal dimension of the policy space; positions on moral policy are shown as position on the vertical dimension.

The fact that we have not considered the position of the parties on the moral policy dimension is reflected in the fact that they are all, in effect, given the same policy on this dimension in Figure 6.6. If voters, however, have preferences in relation to both dimensions of ideology, then they may have ideal policy positions that can be found anywhere in this two-dimensional space. Voters who simultaneously favour left-wing economic polices and liberal moral policies will be found in the south-western segment of the space. Voters who favour both right-wing economic policies and liberal moral policies will be found in the south-eastern segment, and so on. Because the parties in Figure 6.6 do not differ on moral policy, however, voters have no basis for choosing between the parties on the basis of their own positions on moral issues. The parties only differ on economic policy, so that economic policy differences can be the only ones affecting which party a voter supports. Voters closer to Party A on economic policy than to any other party vote for Party A; voters closer to Party B vote for Party B; and so on.

The group of voters who are closer to Party A than to any other party can be seen in Figure 6.6 as those who are to the left of the dotted line bisecting the line between A and B – this is labelled 'a\b' in Figure 6.6. No matter how liberal or conservative they are on moral issues, and even if they are

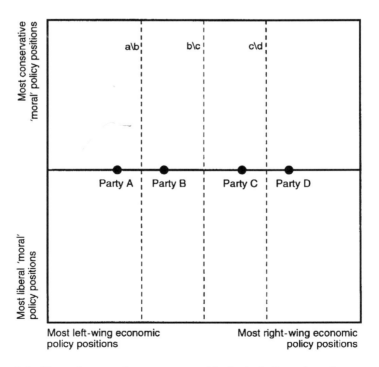

Figure 6.6  *Voters have preferences on two ideological dimensions, but parties differ only on one*

quite a long way overall from Party A, voters are still closer to A than to any other party if they are on the left-hand side of a\b. By the same token, voters who are closer to Party D than to any other party are on the right-hand side of c\d, the dotted line bisecting the line between C and D. Voters who are closer to Party B than to Party C are to the left of b\c. Thus voters who are closer to Party B than to either Party A or Party C are located to the right of a\b and to the left of b\c. Similarly, voters closer to Party C than to any other party are between b\c and c\d. The three dotted lines thus carve up the ideological space into four areas, each area defining the preferences of a group of voters who are closer to one particular party than to any other. We might think of such an area as the ideological 'territory' of the party concerned.

Now imagine that the four parties, recognizing the importance of moral policy to the voters and wanting to offer polices that will attract votes, also stake out policy positions on the moral policy dimension. These positions might be those shown by the black dots beside the party labels in Figure 6.7. Parties A and D promote relatively liberal positions; Party C promotes a conservative position; Party B promotes a middle-of-the-road position.

Identifying the ideological territory of each party is now more complicated, though precisely the same principles apply as in the one-dimensional

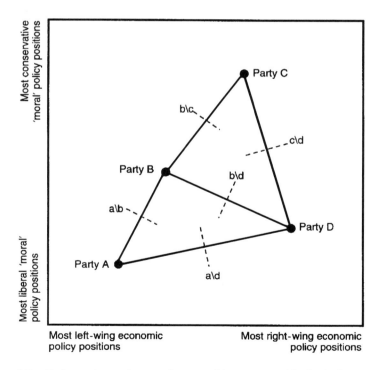

Figure 6.7  *Both parties and voters have positions on two ideological dimensions*

case. Voters closer to Party A than to Party B, taking both dimensions of policy into account, are on Party A's side of the dotted line, a\b, bisecting the line between A and B; voters closer to Party B than Party A are on the other side of this line. Voters closer to one of any pair of parties can be identified in the same way although, because the set of party positions is in a two-dimensional configuration, it is now possible for more pairs of parties to be 'next' to each other. Thus voters closer to Party A than to Party D are on A's side of the dotted line a\d. The similarities between Parties A and D on moral policy now mean that they are 'next' to each other in this sense. This network of lines draws the boundary of each party's ideological territory. The full extent of these territories is shown in Figure 6.8.

Each party is at the heart of some ideological territory, and this territory defines the set of voters whose ideal policy position is closer to that party's policy than to the policy of any other party. Thus, to take Party D as an example, the party sits at the heart of a territory of voters who are simultaneously closer to Party D than they are to Party A (shown by line a\d), to Party B (shown by line b\d) and to Party C (shown by line c\d). The territories of each of the other parties is identified in a similar manner.

Even a quick glance at Figure 6.8, which makes no particular assumptions about the distribution of voters' ideal policy positions, makes it clear that the analysis of policy-based party competition is much more complex when two

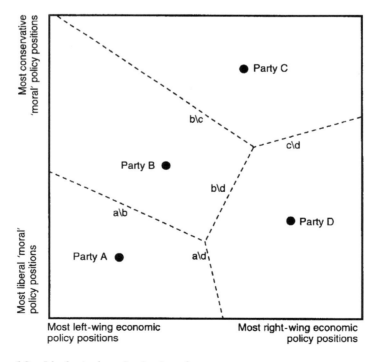

Figure 6.8   *Ideological territories in a four-party system*

dimensions of ideology are important than when there is only one. The addition of more independent dimensions of ideology, for a fixed set of parties, makes it possible for more pairs of parties to be ideological 'neighbours', and hence to be in competition with each other on some aspect of policy. Thus, when we considered only one dimension of ideology small changes in the position of Party D only impinged upon Party C, its sole ideological neighbour and hence main rival for votes. Now that we are considering two dimensions, Figure 6.8 shows that Party D is a neighbour of each of the other parties – its ideological territory borders that of each of the others and hence it is in competition for votes with each. Small movements in the ideological position of Party D now impinge upon the support of all other parties.

The actual or anticipated entry of a new competitor is also more complicated to analyse when two dimensions of ideology are important, as Figure 6.9 shows. Here the parties are evaluating the impact of the potential entry of a new party, Party E, with a centrist economic message but a very liberal policy on moral issues.

Redrawing the ideological territories to see what they would look like if Party E should enter the fray, we see, as might be expected, that Parties A and D are the main losers, and that Party C is unaffected. Rather less expected is that Party E is also likely to nibble into the ideological territory

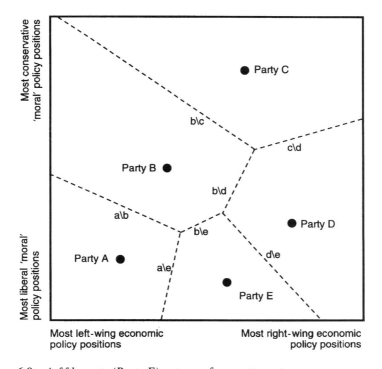

Figure 6.9   *A fifth party (Party E) enters a four-party system*

of Party B, attracting a pool of voters located between Party A and Party D who had previously found that Party B was their closest party. If the parties adjust their policy positions in an attempt to head off the entry of new competitors for votes, then the calculations they must make are similarly complex.

There is no reason to confine our description of party competition to two independent dimensions of ideology – any number can in theory be considered if these really are important to how people choose between parties when they cast their votes. If a third dimension is important, for example an ideological dimension of issues relating to the environment, then we can still visualize the positions of parties and voters in terms of a physical space. We add this third dimension to the other two, at right angles to both, and we have a three-dimensional ideological space, such as the one shown in Figure 6.10. Party D's policy position is shown in terms of its position on each of the three salient dimensions of ideology. (If we think of the ideological space as a room, Party D's position is described, just as we describe the position of anything in the room, in terms of its position from each of the walls and its height off the floor.) All other party positions can be described in the same way, and their ideological territories will now be three-dimensional volumes instead of two-dimensional areas.

A fourth, fifth or sixth independent dimension of ideology may also be important to voters at election time. Just because we live in three-dimensional space and find it hard to visualize pictures drawn in more than three dimensions, this is no reason to suppose that people will not have many different things on their minds when it comes to deciding how to vote. We are now confined to mathematical descriptions of party competition and cannot draw nice pictures, but the essential logical of the analysis is just the same.

This is not the place to give ourselves up to the fascinating detail of analysing party competition in multidimensional ideological spaces. It is not hard to see, however, that things might be much more unstable when more dimensions of policy are important (there are more small changes in party positions that can disturb a delicately poised equilibrium), and how political equilibrium may well depend even more crucially on factors that might constrain parties from ranging wild and free all over the policy space in search of votes (factors such as differential turnout, the policy-specific availability of resources, or the need for longer-term credibility).

The bottom line in all of this is that, if we ignore everything except the policy positions of the various parties, then policy-based competition for votes seems likely to be either degenerate, with parties bunching together at very similar positions in a very implausible-looking manner, or unstable, with parties changing policy continuously in a permanent series of actions and reactions in the quest for the largest possible number of votes. What this shows us is that it is the *constraints* on the choice of policy positions by politicians, constraints such as resource flows and credibility, that give shape

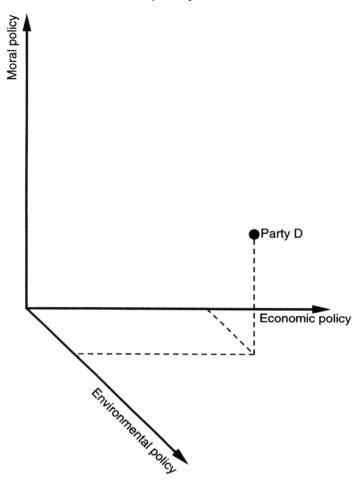

Figure 6.10   *An ideological space with three independent dimensions of ideology*

to the actual competition between political parties that we tend to observe in the real world.

## Conclusion

So it is practical real world constraints upon party competition, rather than what we might think of as the 'raw' underlying logical structure of the interaction of political actors, that tend to be responsible for outcomes of particular interactions. In this sense the spatial model of party competition that has been introduced in this chapter is really a general logical technology rather than a substantive political theory.

Particularly as it has developed into an approach that can comprehend a range of different dimensions of policy that people might feel to be important when choosing between parties at election time, this technology does not give us a simple generic answer about what a three-party system, a four-party system, a five-party system or a whatever-party system should actually look like. The search for such generic answers was what with the benefit of hindsight can be seen to be the rather naive project of those who originally took their cue from Downs in the first flush of enthusiasm for *An Economic Theory of Democracy*.

Instead, this approach provides us with a general way of talking about party competition in a specific setting. And it *is* quite basic and general, even if its methods and techniques can sometimes seem very specific and complex.

If people are interested at all in policy, then they should indeed feel closer to some people than to others, in policy terms. They should comprehend, even if only implicitly, the sense of what it means to move closer to, or further away from, some other policy position. At its most fundamental, the spatial way of looking at party competition says no more than this. If some readers find that the explicit analogy with physical space used by most writers to describe the model with pictures actually confuses more than it clarifies, then they should abandon the idea of physical space and stick with the notions of closeness, distance and movement in policy terms that are hard to get away from once we admit that policy is important to people when they make political choices.

Building on these very general notions of policy distance and movement, the essence of the rational choice account of party competition is the logic of the interaction of two distinct sets of political actors – voters who choose between different policy positions that are offered to them, and politicians who offer a range of policy positions to voters. The basic model is hardly any more than this.

Refinements to the model, few of which have been worked out with any degree of comprehensiveness, add new types of actor (people who supply resources to political parties, for example), new strategic issues (whether or not the promises made by politicians are credible, for example), or a wider political context (what happens if politicians and voters take account during elections of the coalition bargaining that they expect to take place afterwards, for example). The real value of the 'unrefined' spatial model of party competition is thus not that it is a particularly interesting model in its own right, but that it provides the logical engine that can be used to drive analyses of these more inherently interesting aspects of the process, showing how substantive features of some particular situation can condition the outcomes that are likely to emerge.

# 7

# The Politics of Coalition

If a single party wins the support of a faction or factions controlling a majority of coercive resources in the public at large, then it is clearly in a position to take over the incumbency. If we have the ethos of 'liberal democracies' in mind, then we may think in the discussion that follows that such a majority is denominated symbolically in terms of votes cast at an election, but there is no need to restrict our view in this way. For this reason I will often speak simply of 'a majority', to encompass the more general notion of a set of factions in the public able to dominate the entire group, rather than 'a majority of voters'. As we saw in Chapter 4, it may also be possible for a party that does not win the support of a majority to hold on to the incumbency, typically if it faces a divided or disorganized opposition. I will return to this matter shortly but for the moment consider the possibility that no party controls a majority, and that it is necessary to form an alliance, or coalition, of parties in order to be able to control the incumbency and produce a viable package of political services.

The analysis of coalitions has fascinated political scientists for many years, drawing on a tradition of work that can be traced to the early contributions of William Riker (1962). Much of this has been extensively reviewed elsewhere, and I shall discuss here only those matters that bear directly on the arguments in the preceding chapters. (See Laver and Schofield, 1990 for a general review of the field, and Laver and Shepsle, 1996 for an updated view as a precursor to the development of a particular model.) The first stage in this discussion is to recapitulate some of the assumptions we have made, and the conclusions we have drawn, about the incentives facing politicians who make policy promises to members of the public in order to get into office. After this, we move on to consider the politics of coalition proper – the interaction of politicians who are in essential competition with each other to take control of scarce resources, but who must nonetheless co-operate before they can do so.

## Revisiting the motivations of politicians

We assumed that the performance of incumbent politicians will subsequently be assessed by members of the public. This assessment will take place in the knowledge that incumbents have incentives to shirk in office in two particular ways. They have an incentive to do less than they promised, as a result of laziness, inefficiency or a calculated decision to give short change.

And they have an incentive to substitute aspects of their own private desires for elements of the policy package that they promised. Incumbents may develop a reputation for unreliability if they are caught shirking in these ways, reducing the credibility of subsequent promises they may make and hence their ability to attract support in the future. Having promised members of the public to enact a particular policy package if they get into office, therefore, politicians do have some incentive to honour such promises when they have the opportunity to do so. If they do not, they may face a short career in politics. In other words, even politicians who personally have no interest whatsoever in the policy packages they promote for purely entre-preneurial reasons have an incentive to implement these, almost as if they really do care about them, when they become incumbents.

We saw when discussing party competition that, while a professional political entrepreneur might promise wildly different policy packages at different points in time and implement each of these to the letter without personal regard to their substantive content, members of the public may distrust this type of behaviour. The reason for this mistrust derives from the politician's ability to shirk on the job, and particularly the ability to substitute private desires for public promises. This makes it more likely that voters will trust politicians who do not appear to promise whatever it takes to get elected, but who appear instead to have personal preferences close to the policy packages they are promising. A politician whose policy promises differ wildly from time to time is either not promising policies close to his or her own heart, or is having frequent and radical changes of heart. Neither possibility increases the confidence of members of the public that promises made will not be quietly ignored should the opportunity arise. Thus it may well help politicians if they try, as far as possible, to promote policies that they do actually care about, or at least consistently to give the impression over a long period of time of caring about them. (This argument is analogous to one made by Nozick, 1993: Ch. 1, about the value to an individual of behaving in a principled manner.) In effect, the fact that politicians compete for office on the basis of policy promises made over a sequence of elections and incumbencies means that it is worthwhile for them to develop longer-term *policy reputations*.

These reputations may represent genuine private desires on the part of politicians, or they may be a form of self-conscious policy 'branding' on their part. Such 'brands' may be policy packages that are consistently promoted as part of the politician's stock-in-trade, and in this way can become reputational resources that a politician would be loath to com-promise by making dramatic shifts in policy position. Either way, the politician becomes associated over time with a relatively well articulated policy position, from which it is costly to deviate in office. For some politicians, these costs may have to do with intrinsic personal preferences; but they will also be important for all politicians who have an instrumental concern for their reputation in anticipated future contests for power.

It is worth noting that this interpretation of the importance of policy for politicians, as a feature of a reputation that develops over a sequence of contests for power and subsequent incumbencies, is not the one that is conventionally used by many existing theories in this field. This is because these theories do not yet deal with the continuous sequence of election, coalition formation, policy implementation, election, coalition formation, policy implementation . . . that characterizes real party competition. The development and cherishing of policy reputations, which seems to me to be one of the more plausible interpretations of the role of policy in party competition, only make sense in terms of this sequence of events, however. In relation to the politics of liberal democracies, this is a good example of why we need to consider party competition as a whole, looking at the impact of elections on the politics of coalition and on future elections, as well as at the impact of the politics of coalition on elections and future government formations. Only then can we reconcile the popular image of the cynical 'office-seeking' politician, who will say anything to get into power, with the great stability of policy dimensions and policy positions that we actually observe in practice. In this sense the popular distinction between office-seeking and policy-seeking politicians is something of an artefact of the one-shot approach still used by many modern models of party competition.

Finally, we saw when discussing the entry of new actors into party competition that pressure groups of voters may have an incentive either actually to enter the fray, or to threaten to do so, for reasons that have purely to do with forcing other parties to implement specific policies. Some of these entryists may even find themselves in a position to become part of the incumbency, and will as they do so be politicians who really do care about the policies that they are promoting. Strictly speaking, of course, such politicians may not care about the *precise policies they are promoting in public*, since the substance of these public positions may well be chosen strategically. Perhaps, for example, public policy positions will be more extreme than those that are really desired, so as to have the desired net effect, after coalition bargaining, on the system as a whole. The key, however, is that some politicians may *really* be motivated by policy as they set out to bargain their way into office, rather than being professionals for whom policy is no more than a stock-in-trade.

Taking all of these aspects of the motivations of politicians together, it seems clear that public policy positions will be of considerable importance. These positions may be personally important to the politicians concerned if they are ideological entryists, or if they opt to promote packages that are dear to their own hearts so they can do what they like in office while both pleasing themselves and reassuring their supporters. Or policy positions may be professional political brands developed by politicians as part of the reputations on which they trade. Either way, the importance of policy for the politics of coalition is that it will be costly for politicians to go into incumbent coalitions which enact policies that differ from those which they previously promised.

## Minimal winning coalitions

When no one party controls a majority, parties need to forge alliances in order to take over the incumbency. They will need to bargain with each other in order to do this. What, precisely, they bargain about will of course be determined by their motivations. Most political scientists who have thus far been interested in the politics of coalition have tended to divide these motivations into a concern for the spoils of office, on the one hand, and a concern for policy on the other, although, as we have just seen, an intrinsic concern for the spoils of office may well lead to an instrumental concern for policy.

If however we briefly ignore the policy package promoted, as well as the package actually implemented, by any coalition that might form, then we find ourselves in the world of the early coalition theorists, exemplified by William Riker, who concerned themselves only with how parties bargain to distribute some fixed rewards of office. If the rewards of office are indeed fixed, then the straightforward theoretical implication is that incumbent coalitions will be as small as possible, consistent with being able to control the incumbency. In this event, each coalition member can get a larger share of the fixed prize. If incumbent coalitions are bigger than they need to be, then the fixed prize must be spread more thinly than is strictly necessary, and it is hard to see why rational politicians would agree to do that.

More specifically, Riker suggested that coalitions will be 'minimal winning', in the sense that they will contain sufficient members to take control of the fixed prize of office and no more. Minimal winning coalitions carry no passengers, members whose participation is not needed in order to control the prize. If parties are seen as being unitary actors when they bargain over the incumbency, and this is indeed an assumption made by most political scientists for the sake of simplicity, then minimal winning coalitions contain no 'surplus' parties whose coalition membership is not needed for the coalition to take control. Thus all members of a minimal winning coalition are 'pivotal' to it, in the sense that if any of them leaves the coalition, it will cease to be winning.

The concept of the pivotal member is a very important one for minimal winning coalition theory and indeed for models of coalition bargaining in general. As I suggested in an earlier chapter, it seems plausible to argue that only parties which are pivotal should be able to extract any resources from a coalition. Furthermore, a party can only effectively threaten its coalition partners with the possibility of leaving and joining another coalition *in which it is also pivotal and from which it can also expect to extract some resources.* This means that the bargaining power of each party, based as it is on such threats, is closely related to the extent to which it is pivotal in a range of different coalitions. The more coalitions in which a party is pivotal, the more threats it can make, and the more bargaining power it therefore has. One of the very first things we want to know about any new bargaining situation we want to analyse is which actors are pivotal in certain coalitions, and which are pivotal in no coalitions at all. When it is to be followed by coalition bargaining, indeed, perhaps the most important function of an election is to settle which actors are pivotal in which coalitions, something we can think of as the 'decisive structure' of the bargaining environment.

Using the extent to which a political actor is pivotal as a way to measure its bargaining power has some intriguing implications. The most striking of these is that the bargaining power of a party may have only a tenuous relationship to its size, a conclusion with which most people are familiar intuitively and which is easy to show more explicitly. Consider a few simple examples, each of which assumes that, to form a winning coalition, a group of parties must between them control at least 50 per cent of the total weight in the system. First, imagine three parties – A, B and C – that have equal weight. Each party is then pivotal, making a winning coalition into a losing one if it leaves, in two of the three possible minimal winning coalitions (AB, AC and BC) and is pivotal in no other coalition. Measuring relative bargaining power in terms of the relative frequency with which each party is pivotal (this is the basis of the commonly used Banzhaf index) we find that each party is equally powerful, a conclusion that is intuitively plausible. But what if the three parties do not have equal weight, but rather Parties A and B have 49 per cent of the weight each, while Party C has just 2 per cent? It remains true that each of the three parties is pivotal in two of the three possible minimal winning coalitions – which remain AB, AC and BC – and is pivotal in no other coalition. Despite their dramatic difference in weights, therefore, the three parties have equal bargaining power. Intuitively, we might see this as being because Party C holds the 'balance of power' between A and B, and is able to exploit this position. But the simple strategic facts of life are that each party is equally necessary to every winning coalition, so each party is equally powerful.

A further interesting consequence of looking at bargaining power in this way is that some parties may have no power at all. Imagine a set of four parties – A, B, C and D – in which Parties A, B and C each control 26 per cent of the weight while Party D controls the remaining 22 per cent. You can write down all of the possible winning coalitions if you like, but take it from me that there is no winning coalition in which Party D is pivotal. This is essentially because any two of the other three parties (A, B and C) can form a coalition controlling 52 per cent of the weight between them. Party D adds nothing useful to any of these. Take any winning coalition of which Party D is a member; it remains a winning coalition after Party D has left. Since Party D is never pivotal, it has no bargaining power, and can expect to play no serious part in the politics of coalition, despite having almost as much weight as the other parties. What all of this goes to show is that the bargaining power of the actors in the politics of coalition may bear relatively little relationship to the weights they contribute to the coalitions that form. Whenever coalitions are being formed, therefore, it is very important to keep a close eye on the bargaining power of the various actors by looking at the range of possible coalitions in which each is pivotal.

The concept of the minimal winning coalition is a pervasive and powerful one in analyses of the politics of coalition. It appeals strongly to the notion of the rational politician since it is hard to see such a person giving away anything for nothing. In a coalition that has more members than necessary, after all, surplus members are indeed getting something for nothing from the other coalition members. There are two main problems with the notion of the minimal winning coalition, however, which are rather serious and almost certainly related. The first problem is that this notion, almost by definition, takes no account of the policy positions of either politicians or members of the public, despite the fact that these positions are not only important in party competition but also figure in real world coalition negotiations. The second problem is that, in practice, many of the coalitions that form are not minimal winning, but rather contain either fewer or more members than predicted. (Laver and Schofield, 1990, for example, found that little more than a third of all coalition cabinets that formed in appropriate circumstances were minimal winning.) One very obvious reason for these shortcomings is that policy is indeed important in the politics of coalition.

## Policy-based coalitions

If policy is important to politicians, either for intrinsic or instrumental reasons, then the policy packages that they expect to be implemented by different potential coalitions are crucial to their decisions about whether or not to join these. They will be unwilling to enter coalitions they expect to implement policies far away from their own public positions, since they fear this will damage their subsequent credibility with the public at large.

The logical implications of the desire by politicians to enter coalitions that they expect to implement policies as close as possible to their own public policy positions generate a body of policy-based coalition theory. We can usefully consider this in the same way in which we considered party competition, dealing first with what happens when only one dimension of ideology is important, before moving on to consider the more general case.

### One dimension of coalition policy

If only one dimension of policy is important to parties when they form coalitions, and if a simple majority criterion is used to decide which coalition is winning, then the logical implications are stark and straightforward. One party will find itself in a very powerful position. This will be the party containing the median politician on the single dimension of ideology – a result with an identical logic to that which identifies the pivotal role of the median voter in an electorate (see Chapter 5, p. 106). This can be seen easily from Figure 7.1, which shows five political parties – A, B, C, D and E – and their policy positions on a single left–right dimension of ideology. The

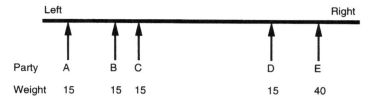

Figure 7.1 *Party D is median on a single dimension of ideology*

first four parties control 15 per cent of the weight each; Party E controls 40 per cent.

Party D is at the median position in this configuration. Moving from the left and adding the cumulative weight of the parties, Parties A, B and C between them control 45 per cent of the weight and it is the addition of Party D that pushes the cumulative total over the majority threshold. Moving from the right and doing the same thing, it is the addition of Party D's 15 per cent weight to Party E's 40 per cent that pushes the cumulative total over the majority threshold. Party D is thus at the median position.

Imagine now that Party D announced that it would take over the incumbency and implement its published policy package on the left–right scale, at the position shown. What could the other parties do about this? Parties A, B and C might propose some alternative to the left of D, but they would not have the majority to impose this, being opposed by Parties D and E, who both prefer D's ideal policy to any policy to the left of it. Nothing to the left of D, therefore, can beat D. A similar argument applies to anything to the right of D. Party E might propose something to the right, but cannot impose this, being opposed by four parties A, B, C and D, each of which prefers D to anything to the left of it. Thus the policy position of Party D can beat anything to the left of it, and anything to the right of it. It can beat anything.

This puts Party D in a very powerful position. Indeed, should Party D be the sole incumbent and implement its ideal policy, it could beat off all challenges. Those parties opposing it would be divided, between right and left, over what they prefer to Party D's ideal policy. Carried to the extremes, this argument implies that no coalitions will be needed to control the incumbency. Party D can do it single-handed, and there is nothing the other parties can do about it. Considering only one dimension of ideology thus implies that the incumbency will be dominated by 'minority' administrations controlled by the median party.

This is the analogue in the politics of coalition of the Downsian convergence on the policy positions of the median voter that we discussed when looking at electoral party competition (see Chapter 6, p.111). If only one dimension of policy is important, and if a perfectly proportional voting system is used, then it implies that the median voter will be well pleased with the incumbent party, even in a multi-party system in which no one party controls a majority.

The empirical fact that most actual incumbencies are not minority administrations comprising only the median party, however, implies that this one-dimensional account does not tell the whole story.

*More dimensions of coalition policy*

As we saw when discussing electoral party competition, one obvious way to add more sophistication and detail to our account is to consider additional dimensions of ideology that might be important both to politicians and to members of the public. And, as we found when discussing electoral party competition, adding those extra dimensions makes the analysis very much richer and more complex.

If more than one dimension of policy is important to parties when they form coalitions, and if a simple majority criterion is used to decide which coalition is winning, then the logical implications are very different from, but just as stark and straightforward as, those in the one-dimensional case. This can be seen from Figures 7.2 and 7.3.

Figure 7.2 shows the same five parties as in Figure 7.1, but indicates positions on two dimensions of ideology, the left–right economic policy dimension and a liberal–conservative 'moral' policy dimension. Party positions on the left-right dimension are unchanged, so that the median party is

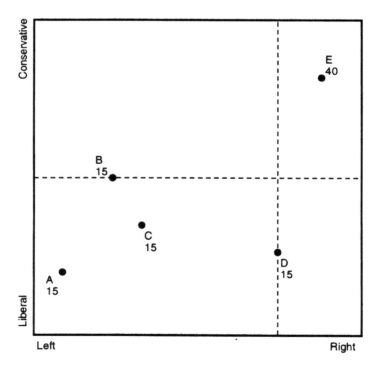

Figure 7.2   *A five-party system with two dimensions of ideology*

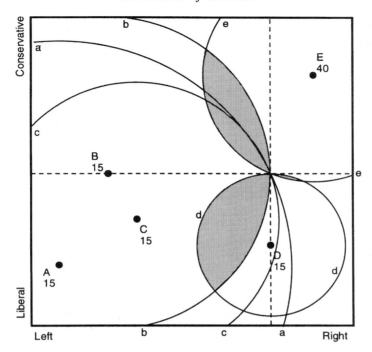

Figure 7.3  *Party preferences on the dimension-by-dimension median in two dimensions*

Party D. We can in the same way identify Party B as being the median party on the liberal–conservative dimension. Each median policy position is identified by a dotted line. The vertical dotted line shows the median policy position on the left–right dimension, running through the median Party D's ideal point. The horizontal dotted line shows the median policy position on the liberal–conservative dimension, running through the median Party B's ideal point. The intersection of these dotted lines can be thought of as the 'dimension-by-dimension median' position. Figure 7.3 shows how each of the parties feels about this median position.

The circle centred on Party D's ideal point is labelled dd and shows how Party D feels about this point. This circle is known as an 'indifference curve'. Since every point on the circle is an identical distance from the ideal point of Party D, this means that Party D is indifferent between every policy position on the circle. The indifference curve dd, centred on Party D and going through the dimension-by-dimension median thus shows the set of points that Party D likes exactly the same amount as the dimension-by-dimension median. Every point inside the indifference curve is closer to Party D than to the dimension-by-dimension median; thus Party D prefers any point inside the indifference curve to the generalized median. Similarly, Party D prefers the dimension-by-dimension median to any point outside the dd indifference curve. The curve centred on Party E's ideal point, labelled ee, shows how Party E feels about the dimension-by-dimension median. Party E prefers everything inside the curve to this. Each of the other curves has a similar interpretation.

Intersections of these indifference curves show how *combinations* of parties feel. Thus the intersection of bb and ee, the upper shaded area in Figure 7.3, identifies a set of policy positions preferred by both Party B and Party E to the dimension-by-dimension median. Note that Party B and Party E between them control a majority. The upper shaded area therefore defines a set of policy positions that a majority prefers to the dimension-by-dimension median. Any one of these policy positions can thus beat the dimension-by-dimension median position. Similarly, the lower shaded area shows a set of policy positions simultaneously preferred to the generalized median by each of Parties A, B, C and D, who between them control a majority. (This area is simultaneously inside the curves aa, bb, cc and dd.) Any policy position in this area can also beat the dimension-by-dimension median. There is also a very small shaded area between Parties D and E, which show the intersection of curves dd and ee, the set of points preferred to the dimension-by-dimension median by Parties D and E, who also control a majority. Taken together, the shaded area defines the set of policy positions preferred to the dimension-by-dimension median by some majority. This is the set of points that can beat, or win against, the dimension-by-dimension median in a majority vote. For this reason, this set of points is known as the 'winset' of the dimension-by-dimension median.

What Figure 7.3 shows is that, if the incumbent administration had a policy position at the dimension-by-dimension median, then this would not be in equilibrium. This is because there are many other policy positions that are preferred to the dimension-by-dimension median by some legislative majority. In practice this means that an alternative alliance of parties can be found, all of which not only agree that they prefer some alternative policy position but between them have the majority necessary to impose this. If the incumbent proposes the dimension-by-dimension median then this proposal can, and probably will, be beaten.

This example illustrates an extremely important finding, which extends to the formation of coalitions between parties controlling blocs of votes the general finding that multidimensional majority voting is often unstable. This is that if more than one dimension of ideology is important then there is no policy position that cannot be beaten by some alternative majority alliance of parties (McKelvey and Schofield, 1986, 1987).[1] In fact the generalized median position is the most hopeful candidate for an equilibrium position that might be promoted by an incumbent administration, since it has been shown that this is the only position that can beat all others, but then only in very special circumstances with no general applicability (Kadane, 1972). For any generic distribution of party policy positions, it is just not possible to find a single position in the policy space that can beat all others in a majority vote.

We appear to have jumped from the frying pan into the fire, a conclusion that motivated William Riker (1982) to conclude that it is politics, not economics, that is the dismal science. This is because, if more than one dimension of ideology is important, as seems very likely in most political systems, then there is very often no administration that is in equilibrium in the sense that its policy package is preferred to all others by a majority. This further implies that the policy position of any incumbent administration is sub-optimal and in a sense arbitrary, kept in place by local rules of the game governing the politics of coalition. The observation that many administrations do indeed appear to be in equilibrium, however, prompts the conclusion that we have not yet got to the bottom of things.

*Cabinet portfolios and structure-induced equilibrium*

One potential solution to the problem posed by the possibility of chaos and disequilibrium in multi-party systems in which two or more dimensions of ideology are important is to look beyond the policy preferences of politicians and members of the public for other sources of stability and structure. There are of course many different places in which we might look for sources of structure, but one line of enquiry has been pursued in some detail by Laver and Shepsle (1996). This is not the place to attempt to summarize a book-length analysis, but a rough outline of their argument can briefly be sketched.

The key point of departure is to note that Laver and Shepsle build their analysis on some of the specific institutional features of modern liberal democracies. It is these features that give them the analytical leverage to look beyond the apparent chaos that seems otherwise likely to beset policy-driven coalition bargaining. They make no general claims beyond this. They start by noting that, in large and complex societies, running the incumbent administration is a major undertaking. In practice, the administration comprises a team of senior politicians typically referred to as the cabinet. A key feature of the cabinet is a division of labour – the implementation of policy in different areas is assigned to different members of the cabinet, who are put in charge of different administrative departments. Pressure of business and the complexity of the tasks involved mean that it is as much as any cabinet member can do to be able to direct the policy affairs of the administration in his or her allotted jurisdiction. It will be more or less impossible for cabinet members to have an impact on policy in some field other than the one to which they have been assigned. It is this division of the policy process into cabinet jurisdictions that provides the structure that induces an equilibrium administration in circumstances in which there would otherwise be chaos.

The reason for this is that it becomes possible, on these assumptions, to forecast the policy of the administration on some policy dimension once we know the policy preferences of the minister with jurisdiction over that dimension. In effect, it ceases to be the case that 'anything is possible' in policy terms. The only policy positions that can credibly be promoted by the administration, therefore, are those that can be generated by putting some specific minister in charge of some specific cabinet portfolio. Since there is a limited number of senior politicians who can hold a limited number of key cabinet portfolios, there is a limited number of possible governments.

Figure 7.4 modifies Figure 7.2 to show the effect of the structure of cabinet government on two key policy dimensions, relating to economic and moral policy. Assume, to keep things simple, that all politicians in the same party share the same policy preferences. (Laver and Shepsle do relax this assumption and look at intra-party politics, but I will not do so here.) This means that, with five parties and two key ideological dimensions, there are essentially 25 different types of government that can form. Both cabinet portfolios can be given to one or other of the five parties – making five possible different cabinets. The cabinet that involves giving both portfolios to Party A, and thus giving Party A responsibility for policy on both finance and moral issues, is shown in Figure 7.4 as AA, Party A's ideal point. The cabinet that gives both key portfolios to Party B is BB, and so on.

The alternative is to give each of the two key cabinet portfolios to a different party – and there are 20 different ways to do this. Figure 7.4 shows each of the possibilities. The vertical dotted lines show which party has

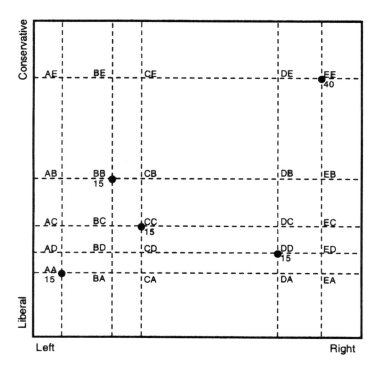

Figure 7.4   *Portfolio allocation possibilities to five parties on two key dimensions*

responsibility for finance policy, the horizontal lines show which party has responsibility for policy in matters such as abortion. Thus the finance portfolio can be given to Party A, and the portfolio with responsibility for policy on matters such as abortion to Party B. Since Party A is responsible for economic policy and Party B for moral affairs, this results in a cabinet at AB in Figure 7.4. Alternatively, the portfolios could be switched between Parties A and B, with Party B receiving finance – this would be cabinet BA. If Party D gets finance and Party B gets the portfolio responsible for abortion et al., this is a cabinet at the dimension-by-dimension median position, DB, and so on. The 25 possible cabinets are each shown as an intersection of horizontal and vertical dotted lines.

Figure 7.5 modifies Figure 7.3 to show how the various parties feel about one of these cabinets, the dimension-by-dimension median cabinet, DB. The indifference curves are of course identical to those in Figure 7.3, but we now focus on actual cabinets that might form, rather than on the entire policy space. The set of *policies* that might be preferred by some majority coalition to DB is shown as the shaded area, as before – this is the winset of DB. We note, however, that there is no *cabinet* in this shaded area. Thus no cabinet is preferred by a majority coalition to the DB cabinet. This implies that DB will, if it forms, be an equilibrium cabinet. This is for essentially the same

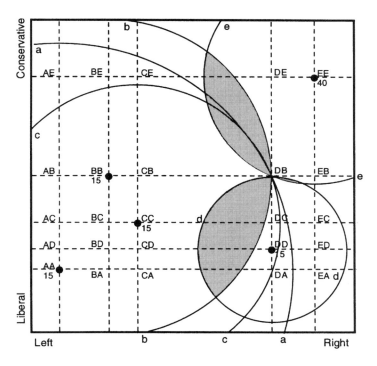

Figure 7.5  *Attitudes of parties to DB cabinet, allocating economic policy to Party D and moral policy to Party B*

reason as the median party can form an equilibrium administration in the one-dimensional case. While other parties all have alternative cabinets that they prefer to DB, no alliance of parties controlling a majority can agree on a single alternative that they prefer to DB. The DB cabinet can thus beat off any challenge and, for this reason, is in equilibrium.

Laver and Shepsle show that dimension-by-dimension median cabinet is the only one for which there may be no majority-preferred alternative cabinet. They also show that it is by no means inevitable that the dimension-by-dimension median cabinet is indeed majority-preferred to all others. The more salient ideological dimensions there are, and the more parties, the less the likelihood of this type of equilibrium cabinet.

Laver and Shepsle also show that there is another type of equilibrium in this interaction, which arises from the fact that no party can be *forced* to take a position in the administration against its will. If a party does not want to go into some alliance, then it can always refuse to do so. For this reason, any actor in fact has a veto over the formation of *any* alliance of which it is a member. Such vetoes can on occasion be used to powerful effect.

Figure 7.6 shows how each of the parties feels about a cabinet in which Party D gets both key portfolios. The shaded area is the set of policy positions preferred to this alternative by some alliance of the other parties who between them control a majority. Essentially, alliances between Party E

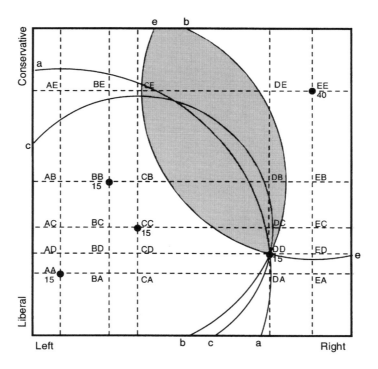

Figure 7.6   *Attitudes of parties to DD 'minority' cabinet*

(indifference curve ee) and any one of the other parties (indifference curves aa, bb or cc) control a majority, but the three other smaller parties do not have a majority between them. Note that the shaded area, the winset of DD, does contain two other cabinets, DB and DC. These indifference curves show that the DB cabinet is preferred to DD by Parties B and E, who control a majority between them; the DC cabinet is preferred to DD by Parties B, C and E, who obviously control a majority. Note also, however, that both the DB and the DC cabinet involve giving the finance portfolio to Party D. What if Party D just plain refuses to go into coalition with Parties B or C, insisting on keeping both key portfolios to itself?

As it happens, Party D is in a very strong position to do this. If it can veto DB and DC in this way, then there is no other cabinet that an alliance of parties controlling a majority prefers to DD. In other words, if Party D can get away with its veto of DB and DC, then it can insist on controlling the key portfolios itself and the other parties will find that they prefer to let this happen than to use their majority to impose anything else. For this reason, Laver and Shepsle label as a 'strong party' any party that can use its veto over cabinets in which it participates to insist upon keeping all key portfolios to itself. They show that no more than one strong party can exist at any time, but that a strong party may not exist. They also show that, if a strong party does exist, it can force its way into any equilibrium cabinet, which obviously puts it in a very powerful bargaining position.

## Coalitions, elections and party competition

When we revisited the motivations of politicians and considered why they might actually do what they promise to do, we placed a heavy emphasis on the role of *reputation*. Politicians are seen as trying to honour their promises in one context because they are involved in many more interactions in other contexts and want people, who are taking note of what is going on, to take them seriously in these. Thus policy may well be important in the politics of coalition, even if the politicians concerned do not actually much care, intrinsically, about policy. This is because they must fight another election, make more promises and have these believed by the people whose support they will be seeking. What this tells us, given the fact that it does indeed seem very sensible to take policy seriously when analysing the politics of coalition, is that coalition formation is embedded in a larger process of party competition that involves a sequence of elections, coalitions, elections, coalitions, and so on. This means, if we really want to do things properly, that we can't analyse elections without looking at the subsequent coalitions that all parties and voters must anticipate, while we can't look at coalitions without looking at the subsequent elections that all parties and voters know to be coming.

Like so many things in political science, this is very easy to say but very hard to do. The mutual interaction of elections and coalition bargaining generates some very complex strategic analyses. An early example can be found in Austen-Smith and Banks (1988), for a one-dimensional three party system. The analysis needed to tame even this very simplistic and unrealistic case is quite complicated. It is not clear how the results might generalize to larger party systems and, given the almost total absence of three-party systems in the real world, this is not an insignificant problem. The most ambitious attempt to come to grips with the interaction of coalitional and electoral politics is being conducted by Norman Schofield. (Schofield, 1993, 1997, provides relatively accessible progress reports on this.)

The eventual outcome of this general intellectual project, which takes us to one of the cutting edges of the discipline, is still very much open. A model that comprehends both elections and coalition formation is certainly a very big intellectual prize, one that has yet to be claimed. In the meantime, a few general observations on the matter might be in order.

First, consider the policy positions that politicians promote. When we look at competition between politicians at elections, our basic inclination is to see their policy positions as strategic. We think of politicians as adjusting the policy positions they promote in order to increase their expected support in the electorate. Electoral policy positions are thus seen as being instrumental. The extent to which these reflect intrinsic desires on the part of the politicians concerned depends, as we have seen, upon the extent to which politicians choose to promote policies that they personally value in order to appeal more convincingly to the public at large. But the essential dynamic of the rational choice account of electoral competition is the modification of policies in order to increase party support, which by definition treats published policy positions as being instrumental.

The treatment of policy in theories of coalition bargaining has been rather more ambiguous, leaving open the question of whether the policy positions that politicians bring to the bargaining table are the ones they really value intrinsically, or the ones on which they have staked their electoral policy reputations. Provided that politicians face costs – either intrinsic or instrumental – if they deviate from their policy promises, the psychic source of those costs may well not affect the substance of policy bargaining.

Putting elections and coalition bargaining together in one model will force us to take a more coherent overall view of the role of policy in party competition. It seems likely that this view will comprehend policy as something that is both intrinsically and instrumentally valued by politicians, with published policy positions being instrumental, being related to intrinsic preferences in some way that allows politicians to present a more credible public face, yet with a clear possibility that politicians may deviate from instrumental published positions in the direction of intrinsic policy preferences if and when they are given the opportunity to do so.

The role of even instrumental policy positions also differs in electoral and coalitional politics, however. There is absolutely no guarantee that the position maximizing public support at elections will be the position that maximizes the likely returns from coalition bargaining. This phenomenon is most obvious at the centre of the ideological space. It is quite possible for very small parties with median positions on key policy dimensions to be key players in the coalition game. Once we recognize that a party must choose a policy position that serves for both elections and coalition formation, it becomes possible that a party will choose a strategic policy position that does not maximize its support at election time provided that, perhaps because it is a median position on some key policy dimension, it maximizes prospects in coalition bargaining. Conversely, as Kaare Strom (1990) has pointed out in his discussion of minority governments, parties may choose not to go into coalitions when they have the opportunity to do so, if they feel that the policy output of the coalition in question may impose subsequent electoral costs. Analysing the policy positions of parties that strike a strategic balance between electoral and coalitional politics is one of the key tasks of the 'big' model of party competition that people are driving towards.

A second very intriguing interaction between elections and the politics of coalition concerns the impact of likely future election results on existing coalitions. Once a coalition has taken office for a fixed maximum period of incumbency, its members cannot ignore the strategic implications of the election that will eventually follow. These days, people have quite good information on the likely results of the next election, in the form of public opinion polls. Opinion poll forecasts will not be accepted unquestioningly, of course, but we can assume that experienced political operators will become adept at using opinion poll data to make their own best prediction of the result of the next election, updating this prediction when a new poll is conducted. Opinion poll results may lead to forecasts that some members of an incumbent coalition will do better than others at the next election. In a situation in which any member of a coalition may be able to force an early election by resigning from the coalition and bringing down the incumbent administration, the fact that some expect to do better than others at this election may cause tensions within the coalition. Members who expect to do well at an election may feel inclined to flex their muscles, demanding more from their coalition partners than before. Members who expect to do badly, and who therefore fear an early election, may be inclined to give in to these demands. Once more there are some complex relationships to model in this interaction of electoral and coalitional politics, although an interesting start has been made by Lupia and Strom (1995). It seems likely that existing modes of both elections and the politics of coalition will be modified as a result.

## Conclusion

The preceding reflections on the interaction of elections and coalition bargaining are an appropriate point to bring this discussion of the politics of coalition to a close. I hope, if there is ever another edition of this book, that it will be able to include a discussion of a unified approach to the analysis of elections and coalition bargaining. In the meantime, we are left with some tantalizing hints about what this approach might eventually look like.

First, we can see that there are quite strong centripetal tendencies in the politics of coalition that mirror those we saw in party competition. In each case the role of actors with median policy positions is crucial. One way or the other, majority decision procedures do tend to reward people at the median, whether these are median voters, or political parties with median policy packages.

Second, we can see that actors who are strongly motivated by the desire to see certain policy packages put into practice can have an impact on these, but mainly if they are prepared to remain out of the political mainstream. Ideological entryists in elections can force mainstream parties away from more central policy positions, but only if the entryists are prepared to sacrifice vote share in the interests of changing the positions of other parties. Though we did not look at this in any detail, ideologically motivated parties can have the same effect on coalition bargaining.

Third, we can see that, while increasing your share of public support might appear to be a continuous function of your best efforts at election time, the practical political consequences of this can be very lumpy once we take coalition bargaining into account. Your vote can increase quite a lot with no increase at all in your coalition bargaining power. On the other hand quite a small change in your vote share can make quite a big difference to your bargaining power in the subsequent politics of coalition. A related matter is that, once we take coalition possibilities into account, certain election results may seem 'unfair', in the sense that they give a small party that did not do very well at the election a pivotal role in coalition formation. Note, however, that this situation only tends to arise when the small party is also central in policy terms, so that the net result of its 'disproportionate' bargaining power is likely in practice to please the median voter.

## Note

1. Some searching questions have recently been asked about the generality of this result (Banks, 1995). Nonetheless, it is clear that voting cycles of the type that generate the inherent instability of majority voting in multidimensional policy spaces are really very common.

# 8

# Conclusion

The substantive argument in this book concerns the political implications of people's private desires for things that are consumed and/or produced collectively. If these things are not provided by secular saints or philosopher-kings, then they will have to be provided by some other means if people's private desires are to be satisfied. Indeed we saw early on that at least one such public good, a 'legal system' that facilitates the making of binding agreements, is essential for the consummation of many of even the most private transactions.

A concentration on such problems, therefore, does not in itself presuppose an overriding concern with the intrinsic merits of collective as opposed to private consumption goods. It simply recognizes the inevitable collective implications of even 'private' consumption of all types of good. The question of which goods should be produced, be these public or private, has been studiously avoided.

The solutions to the problems of collective action to realize private desires are political. They depend either upon relatively informal collective organization, as in the case of anarchy, or upon some form of legitimized coercion, the factor which distinguishes public from private entrepreneurs. I have almost certainly exaggerated this case, presenting the sole purpose of political activity as a response to the need to solve collective action problems. While I would not go to the stake for this position, I do feel that it is useful to see where it gets us.

And where *does* it get us? We start with a very general set of core assumptions about rational individuals who desire things that are in short supply and attempt to realize these desires as efficiently as they can. We assume that the realization of at least some of these desires intrinsically involves collective action. This presents them with a problem, since rational individuals will take 'free rides' on collective action, consuming its benefits without contributing to it.

We see that the collective action problem solves itself in certain circumstances. This happens in two main types of case. First, the collective action required may be such that it involves the unanimous co-operation of the entire group of consumers if it is to be generated at all, as was the case when our nicotine addicts refrained from lighting cigarettes in a room full of explosive gas. The more closely the number of people required to generate the collective action approximates the size of the whole group of consumers, the more likely is this solution although, as we saw when discussing anarchy, the potential for *any* free riding at all makes the situation considerably more complex.

Second, collective consumption goods may arise as side-effects of the rational acts of particular individuals. Thus if people keep their own drains clean, the level of public health may be enhanced. The fortuitous provision of collective consumption goods in this manner is doubtless welcome when it happens, but it would clearly be foolish to rely upon such accidents for the provision of all of the collective consumption goods that people might desire. This is not least because many of the external effects of private consumption, far from being public goods, are instead forms of pollution, and an important form of the collective action, one that many people will value, involves the reduction of these.

Despite the fact that the collective action problem solves itself in these two important types of case, we saw that many types of valued collective action will not fall into these categories. We can set on one side as being of dubious rationality the possibility that members of the group will submit to an absolute dictator who will force them to co-operate 'for their own good'. They have no guarantee that they will not be exploited without mercy in this event, and their own good will rank very low indeed on the dictator's list of priorities. This leaves us with two other possibilities, one based upon the anarchistic self-regulation of the group by itself, the other based upon the role of political entrepreneurs.

As an early rational choice proponent, Michael Taylor, sees it, anarchy involves some form of enlightened self-restraint by members of a group who refrain from taking advantage of fellow group members when it might be in their short-term interest to do so. The goods typically cited as examples of those that can be produced anarchistically are thus those that arise as a result of people behaving one way, when a narrower conception of self-interest suggests that they behave in another. Such goods tend not to require collective involvement in the type of complex physical production process that is needed to produce a telecommunications satellite, for example. Perhaps this is because the modification of behaviour can be reversed more easily than the investment of more tangible resources, while desired collective action involving the modification of behaviour may require something closer to near-unanimous co-operation than goods involving investment in physical production plant.

Even for those large and complex societies that do not fulfil the conditions for typical anarchistic solutions to the collective action problem, indeed, the rational choice account of anarchy may be of considerable value in helping us to understand why people observe norms, which of their essence deal with the modification of behaviour. Examples include people adhering to a norm of honesty by keeping their word when it might help them to lie, or adhering to some norm of orderly public behaviour by queuing at bus stops, when they would otherwise like to barge on to the bus ahead of everyone else. Such norms cannot effectively be enforced by governments or other agencies. In this sense, much of our informal social life is anarchistic already.

But many collective action problems will elude anarchistic provision yet be amenable to the intervention of political entrepreneurs. Since people will never grant absolute power over themselves to some Leviathan, the relationship between the public and a political entrepreneur is in effect conditional. A political entrepreneur is ceded certain limited powers by members of a group, provided that the group is large enough not to be susceptible to absolute domination by the entrepreneur, on condition that the entrepreneur performs in certain ways. Once more, therefore, we see the collective action problem 'solved' by the use of conditional agreements, this time between the public and an entrepreneur. Rather than being 'too large', as might be the case with anarchistic solutions, we note that a group can be 'too small' for members rationally to cede power to an entrepreneur, given a particular prevailing level of coercive technology. The threat of competition from hopeful rival entrepreneurs, given that the incumbent is not all-powerful, increases the chance that the incumbent will honour his or her side of the bargain with the public.

For reasons that were discussed in Chapter 5, competition between political entrepreneurs will encourage them to band together into alliances that we can think of as political parties. For reasons that were discussed in Chapters 6 and 7, competition between political parties manifests itself either in a convergence of the promises made to the electorate on the centre ground or, if entry costs for party competition are low and a variety of parties is contesting the incumbency, in a convergence on the same centre ground by the alliances of parties which form after the election. This convergence may, however, be constrained by a wide range of factors, ranging from the need to raise funds for party competition to the need to have a bureaucracy to formulate and implement complex policies. As we move to richer, multidimensional, accounts of the desires that ordinary people might have, the promises that politicians might make and the policies that might eventually be implemented, these constraints become more important in determining the outcome of politics in a particular setting.

This latter point draws our attention to the fact that most of the substantive chapters in this book have shown that it is often the practical real world constraints on some important interaction of political actors, rather than what we might think of as the underlying deep logical structure of that interaction, that tends to be responsible for the outcomes of social interactions in the real world.

In one sense, of course, this is no more than it should be according to good old-fashioned common sense. If I were to claim that some particular theory could explain what happens in a range of different political situations quite regardless of their local institutional details, you would no doubt regard me as a somewhat over-enthusiastic theorist who had lost the run of himself.

In another sense, the impact of local institutional features on the application of general theoretical models is an important insight that has recently
been quite influential in the general rational choice approach, and has even
led to an evolving tradition in the field that is typically referred to as the
'new institutionalism'. Originally writing on the impact of the committee
structure of the US legislature, Shepsle showed that this structure heavily
conditions political outcomes, and labelled this phenomenon 'structure
induced equilibrium', a label that has since stuck quite firmly and has been
much more widely applied (Shepsle, 1979).

The observation that local institutional features are often crucial to real
world political outcomes does not, however, sound a death-knell for political
theory. Quite the contrary for, as can hopefully be seen from the chapters in
this book, having a good theory of a particular political process is precisely
what allows us to plough through a forest of otherwise undifferentiated
institutional detail and sort out the wood from the trees, identifying *which
particular* institutional details are crucial in a given setting. Without a theory
to structure its interpretation, a detail is just a detail and, for all we know,
may be quite irrelevant.

What this suggests is that we need to look at particular political interactions in terms of two quite distinct elements. The first element has to do
with what we can think of as the 'raw' underlying strategic logic of an
interaction. We can thus think in terms of a logic of collective action such as
that described in Chapter 3, of a logic of political entrepreneurship such
as that described in Chapter 4, of a logic of voting and party competition
such as that described in Chapters 5 and 6, and of a logic of coalition
formation such as that described in Chapter 7. The distinctive essence of
rational choice theory, as it has developed, has been concerned with these
various logics.

The second element of any political interaction is its local context. This
always, of course, provides the data needed to implement an abstract model
in a specific setting but it can often do much more than this. It can identify
institutional features that need to be taken into account by a model before it
can usefully be put to work as an effective tool.

We might think of the distinction between the raw strategic logic of a
situation and its institutional context as equivalent to the distinction between
arithmetic and company law in the field of accountancy. Arithmetic is in
effect a raw and rigorous logic, providing a set of rules that can be applied
in a wide range of settings that have to do with the evaluation of how a
particular business is doing. Two plus two *does* equal four wherever you do
the sum (and I don't want to hear any fancy stuff about the theory of
relativity from any smart-alec out there on Pluto). But whether a particular
company balance sheet adds up to a profit or a loss depends, to quite a large
extent, on the rules for drawing up balance sheets, all of which apply the
same arithmetic but most of which differ in important ways from one regime
to another. The bottom line, however, is that the local rules would not make
any sense at all, and we will have no idea which of them are crucial to our

task, if it were not for the underlying raw arithmetic that provides the logical engine for our deliberations.

All of this is why both general theorists and those who specialize in mastering the details of specific cases are involved in relationships of much deeper mutual dependency than either group typically realizes or accepts. Just as there is no general theory without some real world context to inspire it, every time we look at what we like to think of as the real world, we use a theory to structure our view.

This brings me to the real bottom line. Have the arguments discussed in this book, which are essentially theoretical, added any richness to the ways in which we look at the real world of politics? Ultimately, only the reader can be the judge of that but, speaking personally, I feel that the raw logic of rational choice theory that has been discussed informally above does add to our political intuitions in several important respects. I will conclude by mentioning three that I take to be especially important.

First, I do think that quite a lot of politics is ultimately driven by the need to resolve problems of collective action, and that the developing rational choice account of collective action has been a very fertile source of ideas on this matter. The distinction between the roles of 'outside' enforcers and the effects of 'internal' incentive-compatible conditional co-operation clarifies many practical discussions of collective action in the real world. Given the effective unavailability of outside enforcement in many real world settings, analyses of what helps and what hinders conditional co-operation, including matters such as group size, continuity, the structure of payoffs, discount rates and so on, do help us greatly to understand what we might expect when confronted with a particular collective action problem.

Second, I think that far too little thought has been given to what might ultimately be driving the system of party competition that we in the west take almost axiomatically these days to be the practical manifestation of what we typically think of as our 'democracies'. Given a set of political parties which we treat as black boxes, we can make *assumptions* about what makes these boxes tick and what might result from their interaction. But what does make political parties tick? Treating political parties as political systems in their own right, as alliances of political entrepreneurs rather than as anthropomorphic 'unitary actors', seems to be one of the larger as yet unclaimed prizes for theorists who are interested in democratic decision-making.

Finally, though bear in mind that I am only talking here about what I take to be the really big issues, I do think that far too little thought has been given to the interaction between 'democracy' as most ordinary people get to experience it – in the form of voting every few years in an election for one of a limited number of political parties – and the key political decisions that ultimately affect people's lives. While we can talk in very general terms about representative democracy, what we need is a model that sets out the logical links between the choices contemplated and made by voters at election times, the behaviour of the legislators that they elect, and the activities of the governments that legislatures typically sustain in office. As Chapters 5, 6 and 7 have hopefully shown, the interactions here are complex and the outcomes of the processes involved are often not obvious. While there is an immense amount of work still to be done, especially on the interactions of the various parts of the whole process, the rational choice approach offers us a powerful technology that remains in my view our best hope of finding some way of coming to grips with the fascinating complexities of politics.

# References

Aldrich, John (1993) 'Rational choice and turnout', *American Journal of Political Science*, 37: 246–78.

Austen-Smith, David and Jeffrey Banks (1988) 'Elections, coalitions, and legislative outcomes', *American Political Science Review*, 82: 405–22.

Axelrod, Robert (1984) *The Evolution of Co-operation* New York: Basic Books.

Banks, Jeffrey (1995) 'Singularity theory and core existence in the spatial model', *Journal of Mathematical Economics*, 24: 523–36.

Black, Duncan (1958) *The Theory of Committees and Elections*. Cambridge: Cambridge University Press.

Brennan, Geoffrey and Loren Lomaski (1993) *Democracy and Decision*. New York: Cambridge University Press.

Downs, Anthony (1957) *An Economic Theory of Democracy*. New York: Harper and Row.

Fiorina, Morris P. (1989) *Retrospective Voting in American National Elections*. New Haven, CT: Yale University Press.

Frohlich, Norman, Joe Oppenheimer and Oran Young (1971) *Political Leadership and Collective Goods*. Princeton, NJ: Princeton University Press.

Green, Donald P. and Ian Shapiro (1994) *Pathologies of Rational Choice Theory*. New Haven, CT: Yale University Press.

Hirschman, Albert O. (1970) *Exit, Voice and Loyalty*. Cambridge, MA: Harvard University Press.

Hobbes, Thomas (1976) *Leviathan* [1651]. London: Fontana.

Hotelling, Harold (1929) 'Stability in competition', *Economic Journal*, 30: 41–57.

Kadane, Joseph B. (1972) 'On the division of the question', *Public Choice*, 13: 47–54.

Kreps, David M. (1990) *A Course in Microeconomic Theory*. Hemel Hempstead: Harvester Wheatsheaf.

Laver, Michael (1979) *Playing Politics*. Harmondsworth, Penguin Books.

Laver, Michael (1981) *The Politics of Private Desires*. Harmondsworth, Penguin Books.

Laver, Michael (1989) 'Party competition and party system change: the interaction of coalition bargaining and electoral competition', *Journal of Theoretical Politics*, 1: 301–25.

Laver, Michael (1997) *Playing Politics: the Nightmare Continues*. Oxford: Oxford University Press.

Laver, Michael and Norman Schofield (1990) *Multiparty Government*. Oxford: Oxford University Press.

Laver, Michael and Kenneth A. Shepsle (1996) *Making and Breaking Governments*. New York: Cambridge University Press.

Laver, Michael and Kenneth A. Shepsle (1997) 'How political parties emerged from the primeval slime', in Shaun Bowler, David M. Farrell and Richard S. Katz (eds), *Party Cohesion, Party Discipline and the Organisation of Parliaments*. Columbus, OH: Ohio State University Press.

Laver, Michael and John Underhill (1982) 'The bargaining advantages of combining with others', *British Journal of Political Science*, 12: 75–90.

Locke, John (1965) *Two Treatises of Government* [1690]. New York: Mentor.

Lupia, Arthur and Kaare Strom (1995) 'Coalition termination and the strategic timing of legislative elections', *American Political Science Review*, 89: 648–65.

McKelvey, Richard (1976) 'Intransitivities in multidimensional voting models and some implications for agenda control', *Journal of Economic Theory*, 12: 472–82.

McKelvey, Richard and Norman Schofield (1986) 'Structural instability of the core', *Journal of Mathematical Economics*, 15: 179–98.

McKelvey, Richard and Norman Schofield (1987) 'Generalised symmetry conditions at a core point', *Econometrica*, 55: 923–33.

Nozick, Robert (1974) *Anarchy, State and Utopia*. Oxford: Basil Blackwell.

Nozick, Robert (1993) *The Nature of Rationality*. Princeton, NJ: Princeton University Press.

Olson, Mancur (1965) *The Logic of Collective Action*. Cambridge, MA: Harvard University Press.

Ostrom, Elinor (1992) *Governing the Commons*. New York: Cambridge University Press.

Overbye, Einar (1995) 'Making a case for the rational, self-regarding, "ethical" voter . . . and solving the "Paradox of not voting" in the process', *European Journal of Political Research*, 27: 369–96.

Rawls, John (1972) *A Liberal Theory of Justice*. Oxford: Clarendon Press.

Riker, William (1962) *The Theory of Political Coalitions*. New Haven, CT: Yale University Press.

Riker, William (1982) *Liberalism against Populism*. San Francisco: W.H. Freeman.

Riker, William and Peter Ordeshook (1973). *An Introduction to Positive Political Theory*. New York: Prentice-Hall.

Robertson, David (1976) *A Theory of Party Competition*. London: Wiley.

Samuelson, Paul (1954) 'A pure theory of public expenditure', *Review of Economics and Statistics*, 40: 387–9.

Schofield, Norman (1993) 'Political competition and multiparty coalition governments', *European Journal of Political Research*, 23: 1–33.

Schofield, Norman (1997) 'Coalition politics and representative democracy', *European Journal of Political Research*, 31: 1–2.

Shepsle, Kenneth A. (1979) 'Institutional arrangements and equilibrium in multidimensional voting models', *American Journal of Political Science*, 23: 27–60.

Shepsle, Kenneth A. (1991) *Models of Multiparty Electoral Competition*. Chur, Switzerland: Harwood.

Shepsle, Kenneth A. and Stephen Bonchek (1997) *Analysing Politics*. New York: W.W. Norton.

Strom, Kaare (1990) *Minority Government and Majority Rule*. Cambridge: Cambridge University Press.

Taylor, Michael (1976) *Anarchy and Co-operation*. London: Wiley.

Taylor, Michael (1987) *The Possibility of Co-operation*. Cambridge: Cambridge University Press.

# Index